Implementing a Successful KM Programme

By Stan Garfield

Contents

Preface

In 1996 I was asked by the senior vice president of my business unit to start a knowledge management programme after we visited Ernst & Young's Center for Business Knowledge in Cleveland, Ohio. When he heard that Ernst & Young had a chief knowledge officer, he turned to me and said, "I want you to be our CKO". This made it sound simple, but it turned out that a lot of time and effort was needed to get our KM programme off the ground.

Along the way, I had to endure many ups and downs, enlist allies in the cause to join my virtual team, get executive sponsorship from a succession of leaders, increase investment and commitment to the programme, deal with constant organisational change, adjust to changing technology, migrate from and integrate with legacy software, exercise diplomacy with many other groups, and cope with two large-scale corporate mergers.

Much of knowledge management has stayed the same during the past ten years. The fundamental goals have not changed (see Chapter 2 for a list of 15), the challenges are much the same, and the basic categories of people, process, and technology still apply. What has changed is the technology, the acceptance of KM as a strategic initiative, and the willingness of organisations to assign people to the roles of knowledge manager and knowledge assistant.

We still struggle to get people to spend time sharing and reusing knowledge, it can still be hard to find information at the time of need, and expense budgets are still tight. But there are more people practicing KM today, there are more ways for practitioners to share their thinking (e.g., blogs), and there are building blocks (e.g., communities, team spaces, taxonomies) that are now in widespread use. Emerging tools and techniques (e.g., wikis, social network analysis, tagging) are being tried and tested in KM programmes to better address existing requirements and to enable new capabilities.

The future challenges for knowledge management include creating new knowledge to stimulate innovation, expanding and better exploiting people networks, incorporating narrative in all knowledge initiatives, and making it easier to find information when it is needed for better decision-making. Knowledge management is here to stay, and by applying its fundamental concepts of learning from the past, reusing good ideas, and avoiding past mistakes, KM practitioners can ensure that their initiatives will succeed.

Chapter 1: Introduction

What is knowledge management?

Knowledge management (KM) is "the art of transforming information and intellectual assets into enduring value for an organisation's clients and its people" (from Ellen Knapp, former chief knowledge officer of Pricewaterhouse Coopers). Knowledge management fosters the reuse of intellectual capital, enables better decision-making, and creates the conditions for innovation. This is achieved by providing people, processes, and technology to help knowledge flow so that people can act more efficiently, effectively, and creatively. For a discussion on this topic, see "Defining Knowledge Management" by Steve Barth at http://www.destinationkm.com/articles/default.asp?ArticleID=949.

Why should we spend any time trying to manage knowledge? We are all busy enough as it is without adding the burdens of searching for and contributing knowledge.

If we don't spend time on knowledge management activities, we run the risk of wasting even more time on unnecessary effort that could have been avoided. We might repeat mistakes that others have already made, costing time, money, and even lives. And the results of our work will not be as valuable as they could have been if they had been influenced by the experience and expertise of others.

Here are five key KM activities and the associated benefits.

Learn by doing, from others, and from existing information so you can perform better, solve and avoid problems, and make good decisions. Learning is the origin of knowledge.

Share what you have learnt, created, and proved to allow others to learn from your experience and reuse what you have already done. This provides a supply of knowledge.

Reuse what others have already learnt, created, and proved to save time and money, minimise risk, and be more effective. This creates demand for knowledge.

Collaborate with others to yield better results, benefit from diverse perspectives, and tap the experience and expertise of many other people. This allows knowledge to flow at the time of need, creates communities, and takes advantage of the strength in numbers.

Innovate to be more creative, inventive, and imaginative, resulting in breakthroughs from bold new ways of thinking and doing. This creates new knowledge.

Reasons for starting a KM programme

Why do you plan to undertake a KM initiative? Here are some typical reasons.

An outside consultant advised management to start formally sharing knowledge, form communities of practice, or some other initiative which is in vogue. Management has decided to take this advice and assigns you to get it started. You are told to work with the consultant as the internal programme manager.

A senior manager heard or read about knowledge management and thinks your organisation should be doing it. You are given the task of investigating it further.

Your organisation has some knowledge-sharing processes or tools and wants to coordinate them into a coherent programme. You are asked to take the lead.

Your competitors are known for their KM efforts, and you need to keep up with them. You are told to come up with a KM initiative as good or better than the competition.

Members of your organisation have complained that it is difficult to learn from others, share what they know, find content to reuse, collaborate with colleagues, or innovate and invent. You take on the challenge of addressing these concerns.

Learning about the field

Before starting a KM initiative, you should learn more about the field. To start, read books, periodicals, websites, and blogs; attend training and conferences; and participate in professional communities to deepen your understanding of the field of knowledge management. This is practicing what you preach, and will allow you to learn from the experience of others, reuse the best ideas, and avoid the usual pitfalls.

The Appendix lists 25 books to read; ten periodicals to which you can subscribe; ten websites to visit; details on five aggregators, eight periodicals, six websites, and 60 blogs which offer RSS feeds; 25 conferences you can attend, ten sources of training, 52 of the leading KM consultants and authors, and 42 KM communities, discussion lists, and groups which you can join.

It's a good idea to attend a KM conference before starting a KM programme. After that, try to attend one every year, choosing a different one as much as possible. Many conferences feature training before, during, or after the event. Take advantage of this whenever possible.

When attending conferences and training courses, make every effort to get to know the other attendees. Seek them out during meals, breaks, and social events. Ask them questions, share your thoughts, and exchange contact information. Try to schedule visits with the most energetic colleagues to learn more about their KM programmes.

If you have the funds to engage an outside consultant, you can benefit from their knowledge and experience. If not, you can still learn from visiting their websites and reading their literature and publications. For KM communities, discussion lists, and groups, start by reading any discussions, and then post questions. If events are held, try to attend, especially face-to-face events.

Getting started:
Recommended resources

Book: Working Knowledge by Thomas Davenport and Laurence Prusak http://www.amazon.com/gp/product/1578513014/

Periodical: Ark Group *Inside Knowledge* http://www.ikmagazine.com/currentissue.asp

Website: Gurteen Knowledge Website http://www.gurteen.com/gurteen/gurteen.nsf/

Blog: Anecdote http://www.anecdote.com.au/

Conference: KMWorld & Intranets http://www.kmworld.com/kmw06/

Training: APQC http://www.apqc.org/portal/apqc/site/?path=/services/professionaldevelopment/index.html

Expert: Steve Denning http://www.stevedenning.com/

Community: actKM Discussion List http://actkm.org/mailman/listinfo/actkm_actkm.org

---

Learning about the field of KM is an ongoing responsibility. There is a great amount of content to digest, and new material is published every day. Start with a simple goal such as reading one book or attending one conference, accomplish it, and then set your next goal. As you learn more, it will become easier to tackle each successive step.

The priorities for implementing a KM programme

Here are the Top Ten Priorities for setting up a KM programme.

Put a strong KM leader in place, and ensure that the KM team has only strong members.
Your KM programme will only be as strong as the people leading it. Make sure that you appoint leaders who are respected in the organisation, are flexible and adaptable, are dynamic and assertive, are eager to be of help to users, and who have strong communication and project management skills. Avoid people who are available because they have no current role, who project negative attitudes, or who don't work collaboratively. KM teams are usually small, and having one weak link in a small team can cause the KM programme to fail. Choose team members carefully, and recruit only the very best people.

Balance people, process, and technology components, with a project leader for each category.
Don't let any one category dominate the other two. A typical challenge is to avoid immediately diving into choosing and implementing technology. Technology is important, but it must support people and processes, not be an end in itself. Assign project leaders for each category who are acknowledged experts in that area, who have successfully led other projects, and who work well together. They can serve as advocates for their categories, but should recognise and support the importance of the other categories.

Establish a governance and collaboration process to engage all groups within the organisation (e.g., business units, regions, functions), and to formally manage and communicate on all projects – appoint KM leaders in each major group.
By engaging all constituent groups in your organisation, you will ensure that the KM programme is not isolated from its users. Employees should view KM as something for which everyone is responsible, not just the domain of the KM team. KM leaders from each group should continue to directly report to their current groups, but become part of a virtual KM team. Ideally, they should feel equally devoted to their home groups and to the virtual KM team.

The KM leaders have a very important two-way role. They represent the needs of their groups to the KM team, and they communicate the direction of the KM programme to their groups. They are champions of their groups to the KM team, and they are champions of KM to their groups.

The central KM staff should view the virtual KM team as the decision-making body. It is very important to keep all members informed on current developments and future plans. Avoid an "us versus them" mentality at all costs.

Hold annual worldwide face-to-face meetings to get all KM leaders informed, energised, and collaborating.
Although it is usually challenging to get approval for large meetings involving significant travel costs, it is nonetheless critical to do so. As soon as you have appointed a critical mass of KM leaders, start planning your first meeting. Of course, you are not meeting for the sake of meeting. You need to meet in person in order to establish trust between

team members; communicate the vision, mission, expectations, roles, and plans; solicit feedback and inputs; and provide the environment for team members to collaborate.

Plan the meeting carefully. Avoid an endless parade of talking heads and boring presentations. Instead, include workshops, birds-of-a-feather sessions, interactive discussions, and storytelling. Build in plenty of time for small group meetings, networking, and conversations. Invite the senior executive sponsor to attend all or part of the meeting to present, answer questions, and mingle with the attendees. Invite an outside speaker on an important topic. Give all participants a book and ask them to read it and discuss it in a threaded discussion after they return from the meeting.

By the end of the meeting, everyone should know the direction they should take, believe that their voices were heard, and feel motivated to charge ahead. They will be more effective in collaborating electronically with one another over the course of the next year. And they will be able to visualise the faces of their peers when talking to them on the phone.

Communicate regularly through newsletters, training, websites, and local events.
Publishing the implementation plan is just the start of the requirement to communicate on an ongoing basis. Develop a schedule of regular newsletters, training courses, and events. Create websites and be sure to keep them updated regularly. Regularly solicit success stories and publish them in multiple places. Send KM metrics reports to the senior leadership team and ask that all groups publish their own variations. Make it easy for users to ask questions, and publish the answers for all to see.

Get the senior executive to actively support the programme.
You need to gain the approval and ongoing leadership of the senior executive for the KM programme. After securing sponsorship, regularly follow up to ensure that the all commitments are kept. See Chapter 5 for details on obtaining and enforcing the Ten Commitments.

Engage with other KM programmes, both internal and external, to learn, share ideas, and practice what you preach.
Learning about the field of KM is not a one-time only action. Rather, it is an ongoing requirement to ensure that you take advantage of what others in your field have already learned, succeeded with, and failed with. If there are other KM programmes within your organisation, contact their leaders to find out the details of their efforts. If there is an internal KM community, join it and actively participate. If no such community exists, talk to your peers about creating one, and take the lead if necessary in getting one off the ground.

Subscribe to at least one KM periodical. Use an RSS feed reader or personal home page such as My Yahoo! to follow leading KM blogs. Attend at least one conference or training class each year. Join an online KM community and participate in its discussions and calls. Join a local KM community to meet in person, and create one if not already available in your location. For suggestions on communities to join and blogs and news to subscribe to, see the Appendix.

Focus on delivering tangible business benefits that match the overall objectives of the organisation.
The KM programme only exists to produce useful results for your business. Keep

reminding all KM leaders and participants of this. When publishing success stories, be sure to mention the business impact. When communicating, tie all proposed plans to the expected benefits.

Deliver regular improvements to make the KM environment effective and easy to use. Once the selected people, process, and technology components are in use and achieving results, figure out how to improve them and add to them to yield even more value. User surveys, KM team meetings, external reading and conferences, and your own inspiration are all excellent sources of ideas for enhancements and new capabilities.

When you get a good idea, present it to your KM team, and if they like it, quickly prototype it. If the prototype is successful, proceed to a pilot so you can make improvements, learn from experience, and plan a full roll-out.

Set three basic goals for employees and stick to them for at least a year.
Avoid establishing a long list of arcane metrics. Instead, pick three simple goals which are easy to articulate, implement, and measure. Make these three goals the pillars of your ongoing communications so that everyone will remember them. Set overall targets for the organisation, and key all metric reports to show progress against these goals.

Here are three sets of examples to show the kinds of goals you can establish.

Software company

- Learn by posting questions in a community of practice.
- Share by publishing white papers, submitting software code to a repository, or documenting proven practices.

- Collaborate by using a team space as part of a project team.

Research and development firm

- Learn by searching for previous projects similar to new ones and contacting the project teams for their advice.
- Collaborate by answering questions in a community of practice or ask the expert programme.
- Innovate by submitting a patent application.

Consulting firm

- Share by submitting a lessons learnt document to a repository for each project.
- Reuse documents, code modules, or methodologies on new projects.
- Learn, share, reuse, collaborate, and innovate by actively participating in a community of practice.

In summary, here are the three keys to the success of a KM programme.

1. **Set three simple goals and stick with them for the long term.** Communicate them regularly. Incorporate the goals and metrics into as many parts of the organisation as possible (e.g., employee goals, incentive and rewards programmes, and newsletters).
2. **Keep the people, process, and technology components of the KM programme in balance.** Don't allow one element (e.g., technology) to dominate the other two.
3. **Lead by example.** Model the collaboration and knowledge sharing behaviours you want the organisation to adopt in how you run the KM programme.

Key pitfalls to avoid

In addition to spelling out the keys to success, it is also important to warn about the common traps into which KM practitioners fall. Avoid the following pitfalls.

Trying to take on too much
There at least 50 different people, process, and technology components available for implementation. Avoid the temptation to try all of them, and instead, keep focused on choosing the few which will yield the greatest benefits in the short term to your organisation. Watch out for the allure of the latest technology, the current fad, or the tool which sounds too good to be true. Stick with proven approaches, even if they seem boring and predictable.

Focusing on technology
It is common for KM initiatives to immediately be drawn to technical solutions, including tools, systems, and databases. These can help make a programme succeed, but they should always be in support of a people or process component.

Implementing portals, repositories, search engines, and other tools will not automatically address how content is provided, whether or not people use the tools, or how the use of the tools yields beneficial results. Communities are groups of people, not portals or bulletin boards. Knowledge is shared and reused by people following processes, not by systems. Some members of the KM team will still fixate on the design of repositories, collecting documents, and reporting on minutiae such as uploads and downloads. Keep reminding them that connection is just as important as collection.

Not engaging the constituents
Any new initiative will fail if it does not meet the needs of its intended audience or is perceived as being created in isolation. To prevent this from happening, treat your users as customers whom you are trying to acquire, satisfy, and keep.

Use virtual teams and communities to continuously solicit, capture, and respond to the needs of the people in your organisation. Establish ongoing methods for two-way communications. Conduct surveys, publish newsletters, and maintain websites. And above all, listen to what your constituents tell you, and take timely action in response.

Doing too much studying and planning and not enough prototyping and piloting
It's necessary to study and plan before starting a new initiative, as discussed in this and subsequent chapters. However, there is a time to declare success for your planning efforts and move on. For example, after conducting a survey of existing tools, you may not need to conduct another one. And if you conduct monthly employee satisfaction surveys for a year and find that the results are not varying, you can probably stop doing them.

Prototyping and piloting allow you to test out new ideas, gain experience, and make iterative refinements. You can quickly learn that an assumption was wrong and modify your direction. Instead of planning for a new version of a tool or a website for six months, try making small incremental improvements each week. Users will benefit immediately from the changes, and they will perceive your team as being dynamic and responsive instead of slow and plodding.

Not reusing what others have already learnt and implemented
Knowledge management has been around for over ten years. A lot has been learnt during this time, and you can benefit from

this fact. Reusing the ideas and experiences of others is what you are asking others to do in the KM initiative. You should model this behaviour by applying it yourself. By learning, sharing, reusing, collaborating, and innovating with other KM professionals, you will show your organisation how it is supposed to be done, and in the process, accelerate implementation and ensure success.

Five steps to follow

There is a series of five steps to follow to start a knowledge management programme. Subsequent chapters provide details on each step.

1. Create a **Top Three Objectives List** of challenges and opportunities which your KM programme will address. These objectives align business direction with programme goals.
2. Provide **Nine Answers** to questions about people, process, and technology. This information defines who will participate, which processes will be required, and how tools will support the people and processes.
3. Define the **KM Strategy**. These are specific actions which will be taken to implement the programme.
4. Gain the sponsorship of your senior executive through the **Ten Commitments**. These commitments from the leader of your organisation will enable the KM strategy to be implemented.
5. Create and execute the **Implementation Plan**. This plan spells out the details of implementing the initiative. Contained in the Implementation Plan are programme governance; desired modes of knowledge flow; people, process, and technology component

selection; and implementation plans for some of the components, such as training, communications, and change management. Each one of these needs to be followed as part of implementing the overall plan.

Summary

Knowledge management enables learning, sharing, reusing, collaborating, and innovating to help an organisation meet its objectives. By following the steps recommended in the following chapters, you will be able to plan, implement, and manage a KM programme to help your organisation succeed.

Chapter 2: Identify the Top Three Objectives

The first thing to do is to determine what results you would like to achieve. Is there a challenge you would like to overcome or an improvement you hope to make? If not, ask people in your organisation what is currently causing them the most pain in doing their jobs. Look for opportunities to help alleviate these pain points through learning, sharing, reuse, collaboration, or innovation.

If you can't find any challenges to overcome or improvements to make, and no one is experiencing any knowledge-related pain, then don't start a KM programme. You will be trying to push a solution in search of a problem, and there will be no reason for anyone to adopt it. At the other extreme, if you find lots of challenges and opportunities for improvement, you will need to narrow down the list. Pick three challenges or opportunities for which KM will likely provide the greatest benefit to the organisation. These Top Three Objectives represent the starting point for your programme and the core of your communications. Use them to choose, start, review, adjust, and stop individual projects to ensure that they help achieve the desired benefits.

Goals of knowledge management

All organisations can benefit from their people learning, sharing, reusing, collaborating, and innovating. Based on an organisation's mission and objectives, specific goals for a knowledge management programme should be defined. Here are 15 goals from which to select in defining the Top Three Objectives.

Enabling better and faster decision-making
By delivering relevant information at the time of need through structure, search, subscription, syndication, and support, a KM environment can provide the basis for making good decisions. Collaboration brings the power of large numbers, diverse opinions, and varied experience to bear when decisions need to be made. The reuse of knowledge in repositories allows decisions be based on actual experience, large sample sizes, and practical lessons learnt.

Making it easy to find relevant information and resources
When faced with a need to respond to a customer, solve a problem, analyse trends, assess markets, benchmark against peers, understand competition, create new offerings, plan strategy, and to think critically, you typically look for information and resources to support these activities. If it is easy and fast to find what you need when you need it, you can perform all of these tasks efficiently.

Reusing ideas, documents, and expertise
Once you have developed an effective process, you want to ensure that others use the process each time a similar requirement arises. If someone has written a document or created a presentation which addresses a recurring need, it should be used in all future similar situations. When members of your organisation have figured out how to solve a common problem, know how to deliver a recurring service, or have invented a new product, you want that same solution, service, and product to be replicated as much as possible. Just as the recycling of materials is good for the environment, reuse is good for organisations because it minimises rework, prevents problems, saves time, and accelerates progress.

Avoiding redundant effort

No one likes to spend time doing something over again. But they do so all the time for a variety of reasons. Avoiding duplication of effort saves time and money, keeps employee morale up, and streamlines work. By not spending time reinventing the wheel, you can have more time to invent something new.

Avoiding making the same mistakes twice

George Santayana said, "Those who ignore history are doomed to repeat it". If we don't learn from our mistakes, we will experience them over and over again. Knowledge management allows us to share lessons learnt, not only about successes, but also about failures. In order to do so, we must have a culture of trust, openness, and reward for willingness to talk about what we have done wrong. The potential benefits are enormous. If NASA learns why a space shuttle exploded, it can prevent recurrences and save lives. If FEMA learns what went wrong in responding to Hurricane Katrina, it can reduce the losses caused by future disasters. If engineers learn why highways and buildings collapsed during a previous earthquake, they can design new ones to better withstand future earthquakes. If you learn that your last bid was underestimated by 50%, you can make the next one more accurate and thus earn a healthy profit instead of incurring a large loss.

Taking advantage of existing expertise and experience

Teams benefit from the individual skills and knowledge of each member. The more complementary the expertise of the team members, the greater the power of the team. In large organisations, there are people with widely-varying capabilities and backgrounds, and there should be a benefit from this. But as the number of people increases, it becomes more difficult for each individual to know about everyone else. So even though there are people with knowledge who could help other people, they don't know about each other. The late Lew Platt, former CEO of HP, is widely quoted as saying "If only HP knew what HP knows, we would be three times more productive". Knowing what others know can be very helpful at a time of need, since you learn from their experience and apply it to your current requirements.

Communicating important information widely and quickly

Almost everyone today is an information worker, either completely or partially. We all need information to do our jobs effectively, but we also suffer from information overload from an increasing variety of sources. How can we get information that is targeted, useful, and timely without drowning in a sea of e-mail, having to visit hundreds of websites, or reading through tonnes of printed material? Knowledge management helps address this problem through personalised portals, targeted subscriptions, RSS feeds, tagging, and specialised search engines.

Promoting standard, repeatable processes and procedures

If standard processes and procedures have been defined, they should always be followed. This allows employees to learn how things are done, leads to predictable and high-quality results, and enables large organisations to be consistent in how work is performed. By providing a process for creating, storing, communicating, and using standard processes and procedures, employees will be able to use them routinely.

Providing methods, tools, templates, techniques, and examples
Methods, tools, templates, techniques, and examples are the building blocks supporting repeatable processes and procedures. Using these consistently streamlines work, improves quality, and ensures compatibility across the organisation.

Making scarce expertise widely available
If there is a resource who is in great demand due to having a skill which is in short supply, KM can help make that resource available to the entire organisation. Ways of doing so include community discussion forums, training events, ask the expert systems, recorded presentations, white papers, podcasts, and blogs.

Showing customers how knowledge is used for their benefit
In competitive situations, it is important to be able to differentiate yourself from other firms. Demonstrating to potential and current customers that you have widespread expertise and have ways of bringing it to bear for their benefit can help convince them to start or continue doing business with you. Conversely, failure to do so could leave you vulnerable to competitors who can demonstrate their KM capabilities and benefits.

Accelerating delivery to customers
Speed of execution is another important differentiator among competitors. All other things being equal, the company who can deliver sooner will win. Knowledge sharing, reuse and innovation can significantly reduce time to deliver a proposal, product, or service to a customer. And that translates into increased win rates, add-on business, and new customers.

Enabling the organisation to leverage its size
As an organisation grows, the increasing size is only a benefit if it can use the knowledge of all of its employees. Through the use of tools such as communities, expertise locators, and repositories, the full power of a large enterprise can be exploited.

Making the organisation's best problem-solving experiences reusable
Consistently applying proven practices, also known as best practices or good practices, can significantly improve the results of any firm. For example, if a manufacturing plant in one part of the world has figured out how to prevent the need for product rework, and all other plants around the world adopt this practice, savings will flow directly to the bottom line. By establishing a process for defining, communicating, and replicating proven practices, an enterprise takes advantage of what it learns about solving problems.

Stimulating innovation and growth
Most businesses want to increase their revenues, but it becomes increasingly difficult as industries mature and competition increases. Creating new knowledge through effective knowledge sharing, collaboration, and information delivery can stimulate innovation. If you achieve this and the other 14 goals enabled by KM, you should be able to achieve growth.

Obtaining user input
In order to determine what needs to address, it is important to obtain user input. Conduct surveys to identify current challenges and needs, identify opportunities, and request suggestions. Use an Opportunities Survey to identify current challenges and needs, and request suggestions for addressing them. Use this

survey to determine business needs which KM can support.

Finding out what your users are struggling with, what they would like to see provided, and what they think should be done will help ensure that the Top Three Objectives are based on real needs. For details on conducting surveys, see Chapter 7.

Challenges

After you conduct an Opportunities Survey, compile and review the results. Here some examples of challenges you may find.

Bad decisions: Poor decisions are made, it takes too long to make decisions, or it is impossible to make decisions. The impact is lost business, missed opportunities, and reduced profits.

Poor search capability: It's hard to find relevant information and resources when needed. As a result, people waste time searching, and can't take advantage of information which exists but can't be located.

Reinventing the wheel: Employees have to start from scratch each time they start a new project. This leads to wasted effort, increased costs, delays, and suboptimal results.

Repetitive mistakes: The same mistakes are repeated over and over. This causes cost overruns, losses, and unhappy customers.

Don't know what we know: It's difficult to find out if anyone in the organisation knows something, has done something, or has solved a similar problem before. Any potential advantages from reusing previous experience are squandered.

Ignorance: Information is communicated slowly, to a limited subset of the organisation, or not at all. The result is that people are unaware of what has been done before, what is happening elsewhere, and where the organisation is heading. This is not good for morale, customer satisfaction, and business results.

Inadequate standards: There is a shortage of standard processes, procedures, methods, tools, templates, techniques, and examples. This results in inconsistency, sloppy work, and poor quality products and services.

Expertise shortages: Experts are hard to find, in great demand, and unavailable when needed. The effect is that scarce expertise is missed rather than leveraged, and knowledge which could have been applied to solve a problem or exploit an opportunity is not.

Poor reference capability: Your organisation is unable to respond to customers who ask for proof that you know how to help them and that you have done similar work before. This causes bids to be lost that could have been won.

Long cycle times: It takes too long to invent, design, manufacture, sell, and deliver products and services to your customers. The impact is missed markets, delayed revenues, and customers lost to competitors.

Opportunities

Use the results of the Opportunities Survey, the goals of your organisation, and your knowledge of what other firms are doing to help compile a list of opportunities. Here are some which you may identify.

Speed and agility: Enable rapid decision-making. This optimises the use of resources, increases the win rate, and positively affects the state of the business.

Findability: Make it easy to find relevant information and resources. This takes advantage of available intelligence at the time of need.

Effectiveness: Take advantage of existing expertise and experience. If you know what you know, you can apply it appropriately.

Learning: Communicate important information widely and quickly. An informed work force can act in accordance with company strategy and direction.

Repeatability: Provide standard processes, procedures, methods, tools, templates, techniques, and examples. The result is consistent products and services of high quality.

Opportunism: Make scarce expertise widely available. Applying key knowledge from one part of the organisation when it is needed by another can make the difference in winning a deal, satisfying a customer, or resolving a crisis.

Efficiency: Accelerate delivery to customers. The sooner the customer receives what they ordered, the sooner you will receive the revenue. And the more likely they are to order again.

Leverage: Enable the organisation to take advantage its size. Being larger than your competition is not an advantage unless you take steps to exploit this fact. It can be a disadvantage if it results in delays, suboptimal resource assignments, or inconsistent treatment. The benefits of large size include increased responsiveness, greater range of expertise, and better back-up capabilities.

Reliability: Make the organisation's best problem-solving experiences reusable. The fact that someone has already solved a problem allows the same approach to be used the next time it arises. This speeds up resolution, reduces negative impacts, and keeps customers satisfied.

Innovation: Stimulate growth through invention, process improvement, cycle time reduction, and creative new ways of doing things. Benefits include market leadership, revenue growth, and improved brand equity.

Examples

From challenges and opportunities such as these, choose the three which are most compelling to your organisation to create your Top Three Objectives and relate them to desired business results. Here are three sets of examples.

Non-profit organisation

- Lower costs by preventing people from reinventing the wheel all the time.
- Eliminate deficits caused by repeating the same mistakes.
- Increase contributions by innovating and creating new capabilities.

Manufacturing company

- Increase orders by introducing better collaboration between sales, services, and back-office functions.
- Increase revenue by stimulating a flow of ideas for new products and services.
- Increase profits by sharing and reusing lessons learnt.

Consulting firm

- Increase win rate by improving the proposal development process.
- Lower sales and delivery costs by reusing proven practices.
- Increase engagement quality by collaborating with customers and partners.

Summary

A KM programme must respond to the fundamental needs of an organisation. If it helps address these challenges and opportunities, it will succeed. If it is not tightly coupled to core business objectives, it will fail.

Chapter 3: Provide Nine Answers

After defining the Top Three Objectives for the KM initiative, the next step is to determine who will participate in the programme, which basic processes will be required, and how tools should support the people and processes. The programme may apply to everyone, or to a subset of the population. There will be different roles for different job types. Leaders will need to be aligned to the programme direction. Existing processes and policies will have to be modified, and new ones created. Tools will need to be used, created, obtained, and integrated. To identify these details, provide the following nine answers about people, process, and technology.

People questions

1. *Which people in your organisation need to participate in the KM programme?* In some programmes, everyone will participate in some way. In others, you may target a specific type of participant. The Top Three Objectives you defined will help answer this question. The following dimensions should be considered.

Is the programme targeted for specific departments, groups, business units, or functions? Examples include Human Resources, Finance, Legal, Research and Development, Information Technology, Operations, Marketing, Sales, and individual product or service lines of business. A programme may initially be designed to support only the needs of the Legal department. If it goes well, then additional departments may be added.

Which job roles will participate? Examples include sales people, programmers, product designers, help desk

specialists, shop floor technicians, contract administrators, purchasing agents, loan officers, nurses, engineers, customer service representatives, administrative assistants, and technical specialists. A knowledge base to support help desk specialists is a typical application.

Will the experience or rank of employees matter? Does the programme apply only to entry-level, junior, intermediate, advanced, or senior people? A knowledge sharing programme for new hires to help acclimatise them to the organisation may not apply to those who have been there for a long time.

Is the programme for certain supervisory roles or levels only? Examples include individual contributors, team leaders, project managers, first-level managers, middle managers, and senior managers. A knowledge capture and reuse process for project managers may be designed for their specific requirements.

Does expertise level count? Should only novices, veterans, experts, masters, or gurus participate? A community of practice may be created only for experts, masters, and gurus to ensure that their time is conserved.

Will the programme address specific areas of responsibility? Examples include customer-facing, back-office, and fiduciary responsibilities. An initiative can be focused on linking customer-facing and back-office personnel to improve communication and collaboration.

Is the initiative for a certain type of team location? Teams may be located at a single site, in one city, in one country, in a single region, or worldwide. A KM programme for a team located in a single site might involve regular gatherings to share knowledge, while a global team might emphasise threaded discussions.

2. *What are the different roles that participants will need to play?* For each type of participant in the KM programme, define what they are expected to do. Some will be providers and some will be consumers of knowledge. Most people will be expected to perform multiple roles. Specify the most important tasks for each type of participant which support the Top Three Objectives. Following is a list of roles from which to choose.

- *Leader*: defines and communicates the core values of the organisation, sets and communicates direction and goals, and inspects and ensures performance.
- *Knowledge manager or assistant*: leads and supports the KM programme as a full-time or part-time job.
- *Survey taker, administrator, or creator*: provides user input by participating in taking and administering surveys.
- *Networker or collaborator*: connects with other people as part of a social network or community and helps them out as needed.
- *Community member or leader*: participates in or leads communities of practice.
- *Student, teacher, or training developer*: takes, teaches, or develops training courses.
- *Reader or author*: reads or writes user documentation.
- *Methodology user or developer*: uses or designs standard methodologies.
- *Inventor or innovator*: creates new knowledge.
- *Reuser, contributor, or content owner*: reuses, shares, or provides knowledge.
- *Reporting consumer or provider*: uses or creates metrics reports.

- *Change agent*: enables process or culture change to occur.
- *Process user or provider*: uses or creates work processes.
- *Inquirer or searcher*: asks questions or searches for content.
- *Storyteller*: uses narrative to motivate others to take action, build trust, transmit values, get others working together, share knowledge, tame the grapevine, and create and share a vision of the future.
- *Tool user or provider*: uses or creates tools and systems.
- *Threaded discussion participant or moderator*: participates in or leads threaded discussions.
- *Expertise locator or provider*: locates expertise or serves as an expert for others.
- *Taxonomy governor*: defines and maintains a standard classification system used for metadata, navigation, and searching.
- *Tagger*: applies metadata tags to content so that searches and aggregators will find it.
- *Archiver*: archives content so that it is preserved.
- *Blogger*: publishes blog entries, links to other blogs, and responds to comments.
- *Wiki author*: edits wiki entries or creates wikis to allow cooperative editing.
- *Podcaster*: records and distributes audio or video broadcasts.
- *Subscriber, syndicator, or publisher*: subscribes to news, blogs, wikis, podcasts; syndicates or aggregates any of these; or publishes any of these.

3. *Who are the key stakeholders and leaders to line up in support of the new initiatives?* The success of the programme will depend on having leaders and respected individuals

playing active roles in communicating, inspecting, and reinforcing its goals.

Identify both specific leaders, e.g., the senior executive, the chief technical officer, or the human resources leader, and leadership categories, e.g., all managers, all senior technical fellows, or all programme managers. Then define what each of these leaders will be asked to do. For example, what do you want the senior executive to do? To participate in a kick-off webcast? Send out a message to all employees? Include KM in the balanced scorecard?

What do you need all managers to do? Include KM goals in all performance plans? Inspect compliance to those goals? Enforce them during performance reviews? What should respected experts be asked to do? Lead communities? Respond to questions? Publish white papers?

Answer these questions, and then contact the key stakeholders and leaders to enlist their participation, support, and leadership.

Process questions

4. *What existing processes need to be modified to incorporate KM activities?* From the following list of processes (described in detail in Chapter 8), identify all processes which already exist and need to be part of the KM programme.

- Methodologies
- Creation
- Capture
- Reuse
- Lessons learnt
- Proven practices
- Collaboration
- Content management
- Classification
- Metrics and reporting
- Management of change
- Workflow

- Valuation
- Social network analysis
- Appreciative inquiry
- Storytelling

For example, there may be existing methodologies. Some collaboration methods may already be in use. Workflow may be performed using some technology. Compile a list of all processes currently in use which you can include in the KM initiative, either as they are or by adapting them.

5. *What new processes need to be created?* In answering the previous question, which processes don't currently exist, but are needed? From the above list, identify all additional processes which are needed but are not currently available.

For example, there may not be any process for capturing and reusing knowledge. Lessons learned and proven practices may not be currently collected. The organisation may not be aware of appreciative inquiry as a technique. Choose the most critical missing processes for inclusion in the programme. Consider the potential difficulty in implementation and the anticipated benefits of each in making your selections.

6. *What policies will need to be changed or created to ensure desired behaviours?* Adopting, enhancing, and creating processes will be of limited value unless there are associated policies which require their use. For the most important processes, plan to create policies to enforce adoption.

For example, a content management policy may be required to specify how content is created, stored, and reused. A classification standard which defines the organisation's taxonomy and how it is to be deployed may be needed. A standard procedure for how intellectual property is to be valued may need to be enforced.

Technology questions

7. *What existing tools can be used in support of the new initiatives?* From the following list of tools (which are described in detail in Chapter 9), identify all tools which already exist and need to be part of the KM programme.

- User interface
- Intranet
- Team spaces
- Virtual meeting rooms
- Portals
- Repositories
- Bulletin boards and threaded discussions
- Expertise locators and ask the expert
- Metadata and tags
- Search engines
- Archiving
- Blogs
- Wikis
- Podcasts
- Syndication and aggregation
- Social software
- External access
- Workflow applications
- Process automation applications
- E-learning
- Subscription management
- Incentive points tracking
- Survey and metrics reporting automation

For example, your organisation will likely already have an intranet. It may be using a tool for virtual meeting rooms. An e-learning system may already exist. There may be a tool for subscription management. Using all such existing tools as part of the KM programme will save money, accelerate implementation, and demonstrate the important concept of reuse.

8. *What new tools will need to be created or obtained?* In answering the previous question, you'll be able to identify which tools don't currently exist, but are needed. From the above list, identify all additional tools which are needed but are not currently available.

For example, there may be no suitable technology for team spaces. Discussions may currently be taking place using standard e-mail, and thus not archived for future searches. Emerging technologies such as blogs, wikis, and podcasts may not be available. Select the most important missing technologies for inclusion in the programme. Analyse the likely costs and benefits of each in making your choices.

9. *What integration of tools and systems will be required?* Purchasing or developing a series of standalone tools which are disconnected will pose problems for a KM programme. Users will complain that there are too many sites to visit, redundant data entry required, and overlapping and confusing technology.

To avoid these problems, plan to integrate as many tools and systems as possible. Automate data flows to avoid the need for redundant entry. Purchase or develop suites of products which work well together. For example, add a data feed from a business system to a knowledge repository. Design a website which pulls information from multiple sources to provide a unified view. Ensure that the incentive points tracking system automatically detects all desired actions and doesn't require manual entry.

Obtaining user input

To help answer these nine questions, it is important to obtain user input. Conduct surveys to identify participants; request process and technology suggestions; and compile a list of people, process, and technology components which are currently in use.

The results of the Opportunities Survey conducted for the Top Three Objectives will also be useful in providing the Nine Answers. In addition, conduct a Resource Survey to compile a list of people, process, and technology components which are currently in use, determine the usefulness of each one, and request suggestions for additions. Use this survey to find out which processes and tools are currently popular, identify gaps in meeting user needs, and look for integration possibilities. For details on conducting surveys, see Chapter 7.

Examples

Here is an example of how the Nine Answers might be provided in a consulting firm:

People

Which job families in your organisation need to participate in the KM programme?

- Consultants.
- Project managers.
- Managers.

What are the different roles that participants will need to play?

- Consultants: need to collaborate as members of project teams and communities of practice.
- Project managers: need to reuse content from previous projects and contribute details about new ones.
- Managers: need to ensure that consultants and project managers perform their expected roles.
- KM leaders: need to provide the required people, process, and technology components.

Who are the key stakeholders and leaders to line up in support of the new initiatives?

- Senior executive: sponsor programme, provide funding, communicate regularly, establish goals, and inspect ongoing performance.
- Management team: lead by example, ensure goals are defined, and reward good performance.
- Thought leaders: lead communities, endorse processes, and use tools.

Process

What existing processes need to be modified to incorporate KM activities?

- Project team collaboration: replace *ad hoc* e-mail and file sharing with use of standard team spaces.
- Employee goal setting and reward: add KM-specific goals and rewards.

What new processes need to be created?

- Capture: collect project information and documents.
- Reuse: search for existing content and contacts from previous projects and employ as much as possible in new projects.

What policies will need to be changed or created to ensure desired behaviours?

- Collaboration: ensure that all project teams use standard team spaces.
- Capture and reuse: ensure that the capture and reuse processes are followed.

Technology

What existing tools can be used in support of the new initiatives?

- Threaded discussions.
- Virtual meeting rooms.

What new tools will need to be created or obtained?

- Collaborative team spaces.
- Structured repositories.

What integration of tools and systems will be required?

- Threaded discussions with e-mail and search.
- Collaborative team spaces and structured repositories with e-mail, search, and workflow.

Summary

Planning a KM initiative includes determining who will participate, which processes and tools are required, and how those tools should be integrated. Take the time to do this carefully at the planning stage, so that you don't have to spend more time later dealing with problems.

Chapter 4: Define the KM Strategy

After providing the Nine Answers, the next step is to define the strategy for your KM programme. This will enable you to identify the specific steps which need to be taken to implement the KM programme, thus translating the Top Three Objectives into action.

For each of the Top Three Objectives, list the specific actions which can be readily communicated to the organisation. This will allow everyone to understand exactly what will be done, what they are expected to do, and what's in it for them.

Nine categories of KM strategies

There are nine basic categories of KM strategy: motivate, network, supply, analyse, codify, disseminate, demand, act, and invent. Use these as a guide for formulating your list of actions.

Motivate
To enable knowledge-related actions, it is usually necessary to provide incentives and rewards to your targeted users to encourage the desired behaviours. Often, the first step will be a management of change programme to align the culture and values of the organisation to KM. Setting goals and measurements which individuals and managers must achieve is also important. Establishing formal incentives and rewards will reinforce the goals and measurements.

The means of motivating employees include communicating to them, modeling expected behaviours, establishing standard goals to be included in all performance plans, monitoring and reporting on progress against organisational goals, recognising those who demonstrate desired behaviours, providing incentives for meeting objectives, and rewarding outstanding performance.

Examples include town hall and coffee talk sessions conducted by senior leaders, notes from senior leaders to employees who contribute reusable content, standardised performance goals, monthly progress reports, and awards for those who set the best example of sharing their knowledge.

Network
A fundamental way for knowledge to be shared is through direct contact between people. Connecting to others who can provide assistance or who can benefit from knowledge sharing is a powerful way to leverage each person's individual knowledge. Communicating across organisational silos allows good ideas to be exchanged between groups who might otherwise be unaware of each other. Collaborating within communities allows the members to learn together, which is enabled by community events, threaded discussions, and team spaces. Building and expanding social networks creates valuable links between individuals and groups. Emerging social software supports these networks through adding friends, identifying shared interests, and tagging resources.

Conversations between people are the basis of building trust, gaining insights, and sparking new ideas. Storytelling ignites action, builds trust, instills values, fosters collaboration, and transmits understanding. The World Café process (http://www.theworldcafe.com/worldcafe. html) "helps us appreciate the importance and connectedness of the informal webs of conversation and social learning through which we discover shared meaning, access collective intelligence, and bring forth the future".

Supply

There must be a supply of knowledge in order for it to be reused. Supply-side knowledge management includes collecting documents and files, capturing information and work products, and storing these forms of explicit knowledge in repositories. Tacit knowledge can also be captured and converted to explicit knowledge by recording conversations and presentations, writing down what people do and say, and collecting stories.

Examples of supply strategies include project databases, skills inventories, and document repositories. The content which is captured represents the raw materials. These can then be analysed, codified, disseminated, queried, searched for, retrieved, and reused. A supply-only strategy will not be very useful to an organisation. Even if every possible document and knowledge object is captured and stored, there is no resultant benefit unless there is significant reuse of all that content. Be sure to keep supply and demand strategies in balance.

Analyse

Once there is a supply of captured knowledge, it is then possible to analyse it so that it can be applied in useful ways. Before drawing any conclusions from what has been collected, the content should be scoured to verify that it is valid. Confidential data may need to be scrubbed, or the content may need to be further secured. Lengthy documents may need to be summarised, encapsulated, or condensed.

Reviewing collected information may reveal patterns, trends, or tendencies which can be exploited, expanded, or corrected.

Distilling data to extract the essence leads to discovering new ideas and learning how to improve. Knowledge can be harvested in the form of lessons learnt, proven practices, and rules of thumb.

Sense making is the way in which we make sense of the world so that we can act in it. Dave Snowden (http://www.cognitive-edge.com/2006/08/simple_simplistic_making_sense.php) describes technologies that process large volumes of data with a view to weak signal detection and pattern recognition. Another kind is naturalistic sense making, derived from an understanding of the cognitive processes that underpin human decision-making.

People can also be analysed to reveal useful facts. Social network analysis maps and measures relationships and flows between people, groups, or organisations to improve communities, identify missing links, and improve connections between groups. Positive Deviants (http://www.positivedeviance.org/) can be found, whose special practices, strategies, and behaviours enable them to find better solutions to prevalent problems than their neighbours who have access to the same resources.

Codify

After collected knowledge has been analysed, it can be codified to produce standard methodologies, reusable material, and repeatable processes. Data can be consolidated, content can be collated, and processes can be integrated to yield improved business results. Codifying knowledge also involves establishing the value of intellectual property, adding metadata to documents stored in repositories so that they can be easily found, and tagging content so that users can discover useful views, connections, and collections. Examples include designating documents as standard templates, identifying processes and proven practices, and producing a catalogue of official methods. Refining knowledge after it has been captured so that it can more readily be reused ensures that it is maintained in a valuable state.

Disseminate

Even if captured knowledge has been analysed and codified, it will not be of value unless potential users are aware of its availability. Thus, its existence must be disseminated, both widely to inform all potential users and narrowly to inform targeted consumers. A variety of communications vehicles should be used to distribute knowledge. Newsletters, websites, and e-mail messages can be used to spread awareness. Blogs, wikis, and podcasts can be visited online or subscribed to through RSS feeds. Content can be dispersed through syndication and collected through aggregation, including the ability to personalise websites to display only relevant information.

Examples of knowledge dissemination strategies include providing customised notifications of new or changed content, weekly newsletters featuring new submissions to repositories, and a KM corner on the organisation's home intranet page listing the top ten most-reused documents for the current month. Monthly podcasts featuring interviews with thought leaders, weekly con calls featuring conversations about lessons learnt, and e-mail messages sharing proven practices are also good ways of increasing awareness.

Demand

Demand is the other side of supply. It involves searching for people and content, retrieving information, asking questions,

and submitting queries. Demand-driven KM takes advantage of networks, supply, analysis and codification. It is stimulated by dissemination and enabled by making it easy to find resources.

Examples of demand strategies are expertise locators, ask the expert processes, and search engines. User assistance and knowledge help desks can help connect supply and demand by answering questions, providing support, and searching for content. Specific tools and techniques which enable demand for knowledge are e-learning systems, threaded discussions, and appreciative inquiry (http://appreciativeinquiry.case.edu/).

Focusing more on just-in-time KM and less on collection, content can be provided at the time of need through networks such as communities. By only supplying information which is actually required, unnecessary knowledge capture can be avoided and time and resources used more efficiently.

Act

Peter Drucker is widely quoted as saying "The knowledge that we consider knowledge proves itself in action. What we now mean by knowledge is information in action, information focused on results." The payoff for motivating, networking, supplying, analysing, codifying, disseminating, and demanding knowledge is results through action. Making better decisions is supported by networks and analysis. Implementing changes to replicate proven practices and improving processes based on previous experience are also enabled by analysis.

Incorporating knowledge into routine workflow and utilising processes and procedures can be done as a result of codification. Disseminating what has been learnt allows it to be applied to new situations. Responding to requests, answering questions, and using and reusing content are actions which result from demand. Responding, deciding, and reusing are good examples of acting as part of a KM initiative. Another form of action is the next strategy – invention.

Invent

Invention is a special kind of action. Creating new products and services, coming up with new ideas to try out, and developing innovative methods and processes can help transform an organisation, industry, or a nation. Generating new sources of customer demand, stimulating personal and organisational growth, and rethinking the existing rules of the road can help an organisation develop, thrive, and endure. Failure to do so may lead to stagnation, decay, or death.

Knowledge management can help trigger the imagination by providing a continually replenished source of ideas and experiences. People help bring out the best ideas in each other through their interaction as a part of networks. Publishing white papers stimulates creative thinking. Analysing collected knowledge reveals patterns and opportunities for new developments.

Examples

Here are three examples of KM strategies. These follow the ones provided in Chapter 2 for the Top Three Objectives.

Non-profit organisation

Top three objectives

- Lower costs by preventing people from reinventing the wheel all the time.

- Eliminate deficits caused by repeating the same mistakes.
- Increase contributions by innovating and creating new capabilities.

KM strategy

- Motivate: provide incentives for sharing and reusing proven practices.
- Network: create communities of practice to enable sharing and to stimulate new ideas.
- Supply: collect stories on both failures and successes.
- Analyse: look for patterns and trends in previous work, and select proven practices from the collected stories.
- Codify: develop standard processes to follow.
- Disseminate: publish standard processes to the intranet, and distribute proven practices in a monthly newsletter.
- Demand: use communities to ask questions about how to perform tasks, and allow searching the proven practice repository.
- Act: follow the standard processes, and reuse proven practices on new opportunities.
- Invent: create new sponsorship opportunities, and develop improved fundraising techniques.

Manufacturing company
Top three objectives

- Increase orders by better collaboration between sales, services, and back-office functions.
- Increase revenue by stimulating a flow of ideas for new products and services.
- Increase profits by sharing and reusing lessons learnt.

KM strategy

- Motivate: reward collaboration, submitting new ideas, and sharing and reusing lessons learnt.
- Network: enable cross-functional collaboration.
- Supply: capture lessons learnt and suggestions for new products and services.
- Analyse: select best lessons learnt and suggestions.
- Codify: categorise and tag selected lessons learnt and suggestions.
- Disseminate: send out lessons learnt in e-mail messages, and publish blog entries about new ideas.
- Demand: provide query capability for lessons learnt database.
- Act: reuse lessons learnt.
- Invent: develop new products and services through collaboration and submitted ideas.

Consulting firm
Top three objectives

- Increase win rate by improving the proposal development process.
- Lower sales and delivery costs by reusing proven practices.
- Increase engagement quality by collaborating with customers and partners.

KM strategy

- Motivate: measure and reward collaboration, sharing, capture, and reuse.
- Network: get all consultants and project managers to collaborate on projects, actively participate in communities of practice.

- Supply: capture proposals and other project documents for all projects.
- Analyse: select proven practices from contributed project documents.
- Codify: ensure metadata is attached to submitted documents, and cleanse proposals to use as standard templates.
- Disseminate: make it easy for everyone to find reusable content, methods, tools, templates, techniques, and examples.
- Demand: search for proven practices and proposal templates for each new project.
- Act: reuse proven practices and proposal templates on each new project, and employ customer and partner feedback to improve project quality.
- Invent: use customer and partner feedback to improve existing services and create new service offerings.

Resources on defining a KM strategy
"Strategy of knowledge management" by Steve Denning at http://www.stevedenning.com/stategy_knowledge_sharing.html
"KM strategy is easy!" by Denham Grey at http://denham.typepad.com/km/2003/11/km_strategy_is_.html
"When developing a KM strategy, have a checklist of key issues" by Denham Grey at http://denham.typepad.com/km/2004/08/km_strategy.html

Summary

Motivating, networking, supplying, analysing, codifying, disseminating, demanding, acting, and inventing are the nine categories of KM actions. Incorporating them in your KM strategy will turn the Top Three Objectives into specific actions which can be communicated to your organisation.

Chapter 5: Obtain the Ten Commitments

After defining the KM Strategy, the next step is to obtain the Ten Commitments from the senior executive. This will ensure that your organisation thoroughly supports the KM programme to be implemented. You need to ensure that the top leader of your organisation sponsors the programme you intend to launch. The best way to do this is to create a springboard story to motivate the leadership team, using narrative to ignite action and implement your new ideas.

Look for a successful case of learning, sharing, reusing, collaborating, or innovating that can serve as a good example of what should become institutionalised. Start by looking within your organisation, then to other organisations within your enterprise, and finally to other enterprises. What you need is a simple example of how a KM principle was successfully applied to one of the challenges or opportunities in your Top Three Objectives List with positive results.

Tell this springboard story to the senior executive and the leadership team. If you get a positive response, then present a brief summary of the Top Three Objectives, the Nine Answers, and the KM strategy to prove that you have done your homework and are prepared to proceed upon approval. Gain the sponsorship of your senior executive through the Ten Commitments. These commitments from the leader of your organisation will enable the KM strategy to be implemented.

Ask the senior executive to agree to the following Ten Commitments.

- Approve a reasonable budget for people and other KM expenses. You will need money and staff to launch and run the programme.
- Ensure that all KM leaders have the time to do a good job in the role and are allowed to meet in person once a year. The KM team will need assurances that they will be allowed the time they need and the ability to get together to build trust.
- Learn how to give a KM programme overview presentation. If the senior executive is familiar with the details of the programme, this will underline its importance.
- Learn how to use KM tools and use them to lead by example. To offer more than lip service in support of the programme, show everyone how easy it is to actually use the processes and technology.
- Communicate regularly about how the organisation is doing as regards KM. It should be on the agenda for all meetings, con calls, and webcasts.
- Provide time during leadership team meetings and employee communication events for KM messages. The other leaders need to be reminded regularly of the importance of KM in achieving the organisation's goals.
- Ensure that KM goals are really set for all employees, and are enforced. It's not sufficient to communicate goals in a high-level message. They need to actually be assigned, monitored, and achieved.
- Inspect compliance to KM goals with the same fervour as for other key performance indicators. If KM indicators are reviewed along with the usual

business metrics, it will be clear that they are equally as important.

- Reward employees who learn, share, reuse, collaborate, and innovate. Rewarding desired behaviours provides positive reinforcement, offers motivation, and communicates to everyone how such behaviours are valued.
- Ensure that time is allowed for learning, sharing, reusing, collaborating, and innovating. Part of establishing a knowledge sharing culture is allowing time for the necessary activities.

Culture and values

The Ten Commitments require that your organisation embody a culture with core values conducive to knowledge sharing. Culture and values illustrate the way things are done in an organisation, and identify what things are considered to be important and taboo. Identifying the current culture and values of your organisation will help you take advantage of those elements conducive to knowledge sharing and address those which are not, with the help of the senior executive's commitments.

Understanding how people interact with each other in your organisation, typical styles of behaviour, fundamental operating principles, and the code of conduct is a necessary prelude to introducing a KM initiative. If the culture of the organisation does not include sharing and collaboration, a significant management of change initiative will be needed to start changing the culture. If it does, the KM programme will be adopted more readily.

Most organisations have codes of conduct, core values, and ethical standards which are widely communicated. In the post-Enron world, there is considerable pressure to train all employees on expectations for behaviour, and to repeat this training every

year. Start by reviewing the published values, and then compare these to the observed culture. If they are not consistent, your management of change initiative will need to address aligning corporate culture to the stated core values.

Core values typically include some of the following: delight customers, respect others, achieve exceptional results, work collaboratively, move quickly, be creative, act with integrity, embrace diversity, deliver with high quality, and be decisive. Codes of conduct will usually address how to conduct business, treat customers, work with partners, deal with competitors, avoid conflicts of interest, handle confidential information and intellectual property, care for assets, interact with local communities, and treat the environment.

Actual culture will encompass both positive and negative elements. Positive attributes include: caring, collaborative, cooperative, networked, decisive, egalitarian, supportive, open, sharing, trusting, transparent, fair, inclusive, flexible, credit-giving, adopting good ideas, volunteering, communicative, bold, respectful, honest, responsive, thorough, nurturing, generous, helpful, altruistic, appreciative, pleasant, accountable, and optimistic.

Negative attributes include: insensitive, selfish, undermining, 'not invented here' syndrome, cover your rear, old-boy network, reticent, secretive, closed, dictatorial, waffling, uncooperative, isolated, manipulative, exclusive, blaming, ridiculing, usurping credit, hierarchical, controlling, resistant to change, hoarding, siloed, passive aggressive, critical, making excuses, backstabbing, complaining, and pessimistic.

If the culture of your organisation includes primarily positive elements, a KM initiative will fit in well with the prevailing behaviour modes. If it includes mostly negative attributes, you have your work cut out for you. Culture change will be a critical success factor to embracing the new ways of behaving needed to support KM. If the culture is a mixture of positive and negative elements, you will want to use the positive ones to support your efforts, and use a change management process to address the impact of the negative ones.

People in your organisation will support, ignore, or undermine a new initiative. Your goal is to attract as many supporters as possible, while watching out for, and neutralising, detractors.

Search for supporters to embrace KM, including connectors – those with wide social circles who connect people to each other; mavens – knowledgeable experts who connect people through sharing knowledge; and salesmen – charismatic people with powerful negotiation skills who use knowledge to engage and persuade.

Be vigilant for those who will oppose, delay, or stall the KM programme, including naysayers – those who are negative, contrary, and pessimistic; whiners – those who complain about anything and point out defects, flaws, and obstacles; and snipers – those who attack new ideas, are threatened by others, and who actively oppose change. When detractors are identified, try to engage them constructively. If that fails, contact their leaders to coach them to improve their behaviour. If all else fails, be prepared with responses to the most typical objections, criticisms, and complaints. For a detailed analysis of culture and values, see Chapter 7.

To help create a culture dominated by positive elements, get your senior executive to endorse, communicate, and exemplify the following credo:

- I will practice and reward caring, sharing, and daring – caring for others, sharing what I know, and daring to try new ideas.
- I will insist on trust, truth, and transparency in all dealings – earning and respecting the trust of others, communicating truthfully and openly, and demonstrating and expecting accountability.
- I will look for opportunities to help, thank, and praise others.
- I will eliminate criticism, blame, and ridicule in all interactions with others.

In "13 Myths of Knowledge Management" at http://www.stevedenning.com/slides/SIKM-MythsOfKM.pdf Steve Denning provides an example of culture and values in action:

"Mindtree Consulting launched a persistent multi-year effort to establish five values as the dominant values of the organisation:

- Caring – requires empathy, trust; needed to enable sharing and individual push of knowledge.
- Learning – required for individual pull of knowledge.
- Achieving – high performance requires resourcefulness and heavy reliance on knowledge.
- Sharing – active cooperation; requires fair process, openness, transparency.
- Social responsibility – an outward extension of all the above values.

The focus on values greatly facilitated the implementation of KM in the firm."

Summary

If you don't obtain approval of the Ten Commitments, you will need to revisit the

earlier steps. Return with a more compelling
Top Three Objectives list, a more relevant
KM strategy, or a better springboard story.
If you do gain the Ten Commitments from
the senior executive, you need to ensure that
those commitments are kept. To do so, take
the following actions:

Follow-up to obtaining the Ten Commitments

- Submit a reasonable budget for people and other KM expenses.
- Submit a proposal for the first annual meeting.Schedule an event at which the senior executive will give the KM programme overview presentation.
- Subscribe the senior executive to an appropriate threaded discussion, and ask them to post or reply to a question.
- Prepare a communication to be distributed to all members of the organisation.
- Request time during a leadership team meeting and the next employee communication event for a KM message to be presented.
- Prepare a communication setting KM goals for all employees.
- Request that the organisation's balanced scorecard or equivalent performance indicator reporting be updated to include compliance to KM goals.
- Submit a proposal for a recognition programme to reward employees who learn, share, reuse, collaborate, and innovate.
- Prepare a document defining how time is allowed and can be reported for learning, sharing, reusing, collaborating, and innovating.

Ensure that you follow up periodically to update these actions as required.

Chapter 6: Create and Execute the Implementation Plan

Create the Implementation Plan to spell out the details of implementing the initiative. It will be useful to create the Implementation Plan as a presentation which can be given to leaders and participants in the KM programme. It should be published on an easily-accessible website. The plan should include the following content:

- Programme governance.
- Desired modes of knowledge flow.
- People, process, and technology components.

Define programme governance

Define how the KM programme will be governed. This includes:

- Roles and job descriptions for KM leaders, project leaders, and knowledge assistants.
- Composition of programme staff, virtual teams, and leader communities.
- Objectives and schedules for recurring conference calls and meetings.
- Processes for creating and updating the plan of record and schedules for implementation, new releases, and reporting.
- Process for decision-making.

KM leaders
A knowledge manager (see Chapter 7) should be assigned to lead the KM efforts of an entire organisation, or any group within an organisation. In this role, they will be the KM leader for their group. In the ideal case, this is a full-time job, but in some cases for smaller groups, it may be a part-time role. A KM leader needs to perform the following tasks.

- Improve business results by institutionalising a knowledge sharing culture. With the help of the senior executive and the other leaders in the organisation, take steps to achieve a positive culture which rewards caring, sharing, and daring. See Chapter 5 for details.
- Define, maintain, and execute the KM implementation plan for the organisation. This is the overall programme plan for the KM initiative.
- Define, communicate, and implement people, process, and technology components for learning, sharing, reusing, collaborating, and innovating. These are the core elements that enable the KM programme.
- Define KM measurements and rewards for the organisation and KM goals for all relevant members. This aligns individual and organisational objectives.
- Report regularly on the organisation's performance against KM metrics. This lets the leadership team know how the programme is progressing.
- Implement action plans for people, process, and technology projects. These are the detailed implementation plans for each project leader.
- Lead the organisation's KM teams. These include the programme staff, the core team, and the KM community.

- Manage the organisation's KM communications. This keeps all users informed on the programme. (See Chapter 7 for details.)
- Actively participate in communities. Model the desired behaviours by being visible as a leader and member of multiple internal and external communities.
- Network with other KM leaders. Demonstrate the use of social networks to stay current in the field of KM.

Appoint an organisation KM leader, and group KM leaders for each key group within the organisation. Groups include regions, large countries, business units, functions, and major work teams.

Project leaders
Depending on the size of the organisation and the available resources, project leaders should be assigned to lead the key efforts included in the Implementation Plan. Project leaders should report directly to the KM leader for the organisation. The project leaders should work closely together as a team. Projects will regularly overlap between these categories, but assign one team member as the leader for each, and enable and lead collaboration on a regular basis.

A project leader needs to perform the following tasks.

- Define, maintain, and implement their portion of the plan of record for the assigned area of responsibility. This provides the details of the projects planned and being worked on.
- Report regularly on progress. This keeps other members of the KM community informed on the latest status and the availability of future enhancements.

- Resolve problems in the assigned area of responsibility. This provides the response to users who report difficulties, malfunctions, and unacceptable performance.
- Actively participate in communities. This allows desired behaviours to be modeled and connections to be made with users.
- Network with KM leaders and other project leaders. Use social networks to be aware of prevailing conditions and to be responsive to needs.

If possible, appoint project leaders for people, process, and technology projects. If this is not possible, combine categories based on the backgrounds of the project leaders. Make the extra effort to select strong candidates with solid reputations, since the work that is performed (or not performed) by these people will determine in large part how the overall KM initiative is perceived.

The people project leader serves as the liaison from the KM team to the Human Resources organisation to coordinate all HR development and support for KM. They are responsible for all people components from the Top 50 Knowledge Management Components (see the list of these at the end of this chapter). The process project leader serves as the liaison from the KM team to the operations organisation to coordinate all business process and methodology development and support for KM. They are responsible for all process components from the Top 50 KM Components. The technology project leader serves as the liaison from the KM team to the Information Technology organisation to coordinate all IT development and support for KM. They are responsible for KM tools, including all technology components from the Top 50 KM Components.

Knowledge assistants
Providing a human connection to knowledge sources is important to the success of a KM programme. Relying only on automated resources leaves open the possibility that some users may not be able to take advantage of what is available. Knowledge assistants provide support to users by phone or e-mail. A knowledge assistant needs to perform the following tasks.

- Help users learn about and use the Top 50 KM Components. Provide consulting on processes and tools.
- Facilitate collaboration: connect people to others who can help them or whom they can help.
- Direct users to the right knowledge sources based on their specific needs. Locate relevant knowledge resources.
- Assist users in searching for content and knowledge. Find reusable content.
- Actively offer assistance to work teams. Engage by contacting users, not just waiting for requests to arrive.
- Review content submitted to repositories for compliance to quality standards, and follow-up as required to improve quality.
- Solicit user feedback. Direct feedback to the right person within the KM team.
- Conduct training: create and record self-paced courses.
- Search for information to help meet deadlines. Send search results to users who are not connected to the network.
- Network with other knowledge assistants. Back each other up. Help respond to requests. Take over open requests at the end of the work day based on being in different time zones.

Good knowledge assistants need to be able to relate to others and put them at ease. They should have good communication skills, be able to quickly learn about tools and processes, and be eager to be of help to users. They should have experience in one or more of the following areas: KM, collaboration, help desks, intranet/Internet searching, and peer-to-peer networking.

Appoint an organisation knowledge assistant leader to coordinate efforts between all other knowledge assistants. This can be a role assigned to one of the KM leaders in addition to their other duties. Assign additional knowledge assistants for each key group within the organisation. Groups include regions, large countries, business units, functions, and major work teams.

Composition of programme staff, virtual teams, and leader communities
To manage the KM programme, engage the constituents, and ensure alignment with the Top Three Objectives, the following teams and communities are recommended.

Program Staff: A work team with formal reporting lines. It manages projects, resolves problems, and reports progress. It includes the organisation KM leader and the project leaders.

Core Team: A virtual team, by invitation of the organisation KM leader. It sets the direction of the organisation programme, debates issues candidly, and makes decisions. It includes the programme staff and the group KM leaders.

Knowledge Assistant Team: A virtual team, by invitation of the organisation knowledge assistant leader. It monitors trends, manages performance, and facilitates back-up in responding to requests. It includes the organisation knowledge assistant leader and all knowledge assistants.

Group Teams (e.g., for a region or business unit): Virtual teams, by invitation of the group KM leader. They set the direction of the group programme, debate issues candidly, and make decisions. They include the group KM leader, all KM leaders within the group, and all knowledge assistants within the group,

KM Community: A leader community, open to all within the organisation. Its purpose is to learn, share, collaborate, innovate, communicate, solicit input, and provide feedback on knowledge management. It includes the core team, all other KM leaders, and all knowledge assistants.

For the programme staff, hire strong project leaders. For the core team, influence the managers in the groups to hire strong KM leaders. For the knowledge assistant community, ask all knowledge assistants to participate. For the group teams, the group KM leaders should influence the managers in the sub-groups (departments, countries, etc.) to hire strong KM leaders. For the KM community, reach out to as many people as possible who are involved with or have a passion for KM and invite them to join. Here are three examples of possible group teams.

European KM Team: Sub-groups are countries within Europe and region-level teams.

Human Resources KM Team: Sub-groups are functions within HR, such as training, organisation development, compensation, etc.

Services KM Team: Sub-groups are business units within Services, such as consulting, outsourcing, and support.

Create collaborative team spaces for the core team, knowledge assistant team, all group teams, and for the KM community. Create a threaded discussion for the KM community, and discourage any KM discussions from taking place outside of this forum. Funnel all knowledge sharing, requests for help, and general KM communications through this single threaded discussion. Use it to model behaviour for community leadership, participation, and communications.

Objectives and schedules for recurring conference calls and meetings
When you have formed KM teams and communities, you need to decide how and when to meet. Before scheduling calls and meetings, define the objectives for meeting. Here are suggested objectives from which to select: communicate progress; receive feedback on work; solicit inputs on future direction; educate and inform about new ideas, industry trends, and what other organisations are doing; stimulate discussions; make decisions; initiate pilots; evaluate prototypes; collaborate on analysing information, solving problems, and innovating; and share good ideas, success stories, and lessons learnt to encourage reuse.

After you select your objectives, poll the members of each team with three possible meeting frequencies and durations, and ask them to vote based on their preferences. For example, a weekly 60-minute conference call, a fortnightly 90-minute conference call, or a monthly 120-minute conference call.

Once you decide on the frequency and duration of calls, use whatever technology is available to you to make the entire process as smooth as possible. Consider the following possibilities. Use the integration between Microsoft Outlook and SharePoint to create a meeting space for the calls and send out recurring meeting invitations. Choose a conference call provider who can cover the countries of the team members with reasonably-priced dial-in numbers. Record the calls and provide playback on demand via the intranet or dial-in. Use a virtual meeting room tool for presentations, white board use, and live demonstrations. Post the meeting agendas to the team space, along with copies of presentations and links to virtual meeting rooms.

Here are some keys to making regular conference calls successful. Work hard to ensure that the calls are lively by carefully creating agendas, stimulating discussions, and asking questions. Schedule dynamic guest speakers, both internal and external. Allow any member to add items to the agendas for future calls. If agendas don't fill up, suggest topics and speakers until they do. Moderate the calls to ensure no background noise, adherence to agenda times, and to regulate discussions. After the calls have been held for a few months, tune the schedule, duration, and content. You may need to increase or decrease frequency and/or duration. Don't hesitate to do so. This reflects being adaptable, one of the attributes of a good knowledge manager.

Once your KM community has been formed and has met by phone a few times, you can ask them for their inputs on when, where, and for how long to have the first face-to-face meeting. Try to include as many of the key KM leaders as possible, but limit the total attendance to no more than 50 to keep the meeting manageable. If possible, try to rotate the meeting location between different parts of the country or world. To take advantage of the meeting location, invite as many KM

leaders who will incur low travel expenses to attend. For example, when meeting in Europe, invite the KM leaders from all of the European countries, but only a few key leaders from other regions.

Processes for creating and updating the plan of record and schedules for implementation, new releases, and reporting
The project leaders are responsible for defining, maintaining, and implementing their portion of the plan of record for their assigned areas of responsibility, and reporting regularly on progress. Based on the results of user surveys (see Chapter 3), inputs from the KM community, and the details in the Top Three Objectives, the Nine Answers, the KM strategy, and the Implementation Plan, each project leader should select three key projects to lead. Here are three sets of examples of possible selections.

Public sector organisation
People

- Embed KM goals and measurements into the employee review process.
- Develop and deliver training courses, self-paced modules, user guides, and administrative guides.
- Conduct employee satisfaction surveys to measure progress and identify needed improvements.

Process

- Develop a KM management of change plan and help implement it.
- Define a governance process for repositories and libraries – how content is captured, improved and reused.
- Implement a collaboration process for project teams.

Technology

- Define an overall information architecture and data model.
- Make it easy to join all communities by clicking on a single button.
- Implement a data warehouse for self-service KM indicator reporting.

Manufacturing company
People

- Coordinate a series of regional KM webinars.
- Develop, pilot, and rollout an incentive programme.
- Publish a monthly newsletter.

Process

- Develop a quality improvement plan for repository content.
- Implement a process for creating and maintaining a standard taxonomy.
- Implement a process to identify and designate proven practices.

Technology

- Automate data flows from business systems to repositories to reduce the need for redundant data entry.
- Provide an offline capability for repository content.
- Implement a prototype social software tool for personal home pages and social networking.

Systems integration firm
People

- Improve KM websites and develop new user interfaces that map to different views.

- Develop and implement a plan to improve employee satisfaction.
- Increase participation in communities and threaded discussions.

Process

- Implement a capture process for software source code.
- Implement a reuse process for proposal management.
- Define a process for creating and updating sales kits.

Technology

- Integrate repository search with corporate intranet search and add localised search capability.
- Add external access to collaborative team spaces for customers and partners.
- Automate archival of content from team spaces and repositories.

In the recurring core team conference calls, include a regular time slot on the agenda for reviewing each project leader's portion of the plan of record. The plans should be updated prior to the scheduled calls, including implementation schedule details, timing and features of new releases, and reasons for any schedule changes.

The overall plan of record should be maintained on an easily-accessible website. It should include the implementation schedule, the new release schedule, the reporting schedule, the change management plan, the training and communications plan, the standard employee goals, the organisational measurements, and the standard taxonomy.

The core team should decide on the details for reporting. These should include which metrics to report, the targets for each metric, the format of reports, what level of detail and how granular reports should be, to whom reports will be distributed, where reports will be stored, how frequently reports will be produced, who will produce reports, how and when to revise metrics and targets, and how to produce custom reports.

Process for decision-making
The core team should decide on the details for decision-making. These should include a change request process, a process for setting priorities, a voting process, when consensus is needed and when it is not needed, and a conflict resolution process. Here is an example of a decision-making process.

Change request process: KM leaders can submit requests using a form on the team space.

Process for setting priorities: The core team meets once a month and ranks all current and proposed projects.

Voting process: Voting is done using a poll on the team space.

When consensus is needed, and when it is not needed: Major changes to the user interface require consensus of the core team. Minor changes do not.

Conflict resolution process: The organisation KM leader resolves all conflicts in any of the virtual teams.

Decisions should be made with as much diversity of opinion, debate, and discussion as is reasonable. Whenever a consensus among the core team can be achieved, that is desirable. But when there is no consensus, after an appropriate amount of discussion,

the organisation KM leader should make decisions so that progress is not stalled.

How the KM programme is governed is critical to its success. Without strong leaders, representation from all constituent groups, regular calls and meetings, and effective processes for planning, reporting, and decision-making, the implementation plan can't be properly executed, and thus the Top Three Objectives won't be achieved. Pay close attention to getting this right, and it will pay off later.

Define the desired modes of knowledge flow

In designing a new KM initiative, your goal is to implement people, process, and technology components which will achieve your Top Three Objectives. In order to do so, think about which types of knowledge flow are needed. There are five key ways in which the flow of knowledge can be tapped.

Collection: processes and repositories for capturing explicit knowledge. This involves attempting to codify and encapsulate knowledge in writing or some other form of stored data.

Connection: collaboration, communities, and social networks for sharing tacit knowledge. Connecting people allows them to exchange knowledge by communicating with one another.

Boundary spanning: bridges across organisational boundaries for enabling knowledge to flow between previously-isolated groups. Building bridges to connect otherwise unconnected networks makes available previously unknown sources of knowledge.

Discovery: processes for learning from existing sources of information, including systems, databases, and libraries. Scouring established knowledge bases in order to gain insights, distill trends, and uncover useful nuggets can provide a competitive advantage.

Creation: processes for stimulating innovation and facilitating invention. By using the other modes of knowledge flow, creative ideas can be developed into useful new products, services, and ways of getting work done.

Putting knowledge to work in order to solve a problem, save time, make a sale, inspire innovation, improve quality, lower costs, increase profits, meet customer needs, and otherwise improve the world requires knowledge to flow between people.

In *The Wealth of Knowledge: Intellectual Capital and the Twenty-first Century Organization* (http://www.amazon.com/gp/product/0385500726/) by Thomas Stewart, Chapter 8 'A New Agenda: Managing Knowledge Projects': on p175, Stewart makes the following important point:

"Connection, not collection: That's the essence of knowledge management. The purpose of projects, therefore, is to get knowledge moving, not to freeze it; to distribute it, not to shelve it."

Chapter 6 'The Case Against Knowledge Management': on p116, Stewart describes "the Kraken," a Lotus Notes e-mail list for general questions and answers:

"The founders imagined that people would spark discussion by uploading white papers and the like – that is, they expected that users would pile logs of content in the fireplace, generating fire in the form of questions, critiques, and the like. Instead,

the spark comes first: 80% of Kraken traffic starts with questions: Does anybody know? Does anybody have? Has anybody ever done something like?

The Kraken differs from KnowledgeCurve. The latter is supply-side; it's full of documents, artifacts, and other explicit knowledge… The Kraken's a conversation; KnowledgeCurve and its cousins are compendiums. KnowledgeCurve is about teaching; the Kraken is about learning."

In *Volunteer not conscript* (http://www.cognitive-edge.com/2006/08/volunteer_not_conscript.php), Dave Snowden writes:

"Many years ago I formulated three rules or heuristics of Knowledge Management:

- Knowledge will only ever be volunteered it can not be conscripted.
- We only know what we know when we need to know it.
- We always know more than we can tell and we will always tell more than we can write down.

The first of these reference the fact that you cannot make someone surrender their knowledge in the way that you can make them conform with a process. It was originally coined in reference to individuals, but I have come to realise that it also applies to organisations… So a new formulation, or possibly extension of the first rule would be:

If you ask someone, or a body for specific knowledge in the context of a real need it will never be refused. If you ask them to give you your knowledge on the basis that you may need it in the future, then you will never receive it."

Many KM programmes emphasise capture too much – collecting lots of documents, but not being able to effectively reuse them. So which types of knowledge flow should you emphasise, and to what extent? Here is a look at each type and when to incorporate it.

Collection: processes and repositories for capturing explicit knowledge
Explicit knowledge is formal knowledge that can be conveyed from one person to another in systematic ways. Examples include books, documents, white papers, databases, policy manuals, e-mail messages, spreadsheets, methodologies, multimedia, and other types of files. Based on the points made by Tom Stewart and Dave Snowden, it is reasonable to question the value of devoting significant energy to document collection in advance of a need. But there is still value in capturing some information in easily-retrievable repositories.

For example, before beginning a new project, it is useful to ask the question "has anyone ever done anything like this before?". If information on all prior projects has been collected in a searchable repository, then this question can be answered. Not all of the documents created by previous projects may have been captured, but if the names of the project team members are available, then it is possible to contact them to find out more and to request any relevant documents. This is an example of how collection and connection can work together to deliver important knowledge at the time of need.

Another example of how collection and connection complement one another is asking a community for help. In responding to a request from one community member, another member can point to a previously-stored document which meets the needs of the first member.

One way of minimising the need for collection is to use connection to identify a need and then respond with a document only upon such a request. Another way is to rely on discovery to ferret out information from existing databases such that additional collection is not required. For example, if information on previous projects is automatically captured as part of the organisation's business management system, then it can be retrieved without the need for additional data entry.

Collection provides the supply side of knowledge. If you decide that it is needed, try to keep it to the absolute minimum needed to support the Top Three Objectives. Rely on other modes of knowledge flow as much as possible. And be sensitive to Dave Snowden's point: "If you ask them to give you your knowledge on the basis that you may need it in the future, then you will never receive it".

Connection: collaboration, communities and social networks for sharing tacit knowledge
Tacit knowledge is personal knowledge that resides in an individual. It is content that has not been recorded or exchanged. It relies on experiences, ideas, insights, values, and judgements and usually requires joint, shared activities in order to transmit it. Individuals possess tacit knowledge and must learn to verbalise that knowledge. The art of talking about a problem or opportunity causes it to take shape and to be defined. Once defined, it can be solved or developed.

Dave Snowden wrote "we will always tell more than we can write down". According to Tom Stewart, "connection is the essence of knowledge management". So this mode of knowledge flow should be a key part of your KM plan. Connection supports the demand side of knowledge. It enables demand-driven or just-in-time KM.

Dave Snowden asserts: "If you ask someone, or a body for specific knowledge in the context of a real need it will never be refused". Tom Stewart states: "80% of Kraken traffic starts with questions: Does anybody know? Does anybody have? Has anybody ever done something like?".

This supports the argument for including communities and threaded discussions in your selected list of KM components. Communities are the people who connect, and threaded discussions are the mechanism for the connection. These should almost always be part of any KM programme.

Boundary spanning: bridges across organisational boundaries for enabling knowledge to flow between previously-isolated groups
In *Building Smart Communities through Network Weaving* (http://www.orgnet.com/BuildingNetworks.pdf), Valdis Krebs and June Holley define boundary spanners as "nodes that connect two or more clusters – they act as bridges between groups". They go on to observe:

"When left unmanaged, networks follow two simple, yet powerful driving forces: (1) Birds of a feather flock together. (2) Those close by, form a tie. This results in many small and dense clusters with little or no diversity. Everyone in the cluster knows what everyone else knows and no one knows what is going on in other clusters. The lack of outside information, and dense cohesion within the network, removes all possibility for new ideas and innovations."

To overcome this tendency, it is important to make explicit efforts to establish links between different groups. Examples include different regions of the world (e.g., North America, Latin America, Europe/Middle East/Africa, and Asia Pacific), functions (e.g., engineering, manufacturing, marketing, sales, logistics, and service), business units (e.g., paper products, cleaning products, and health products), roles (e.g., interns, retirees, and contractors), and organisations (e.g., employees, customers, and partners).

An example of how boundary spanning can help overcome organisational barriers is product development and introduction. Marketing tells Engineering to develop a new product to meet a customer need. Engineering designs the product, which is produced by Manufacturing. Marketing promotes the product, which is sold to customers by Sales and delivered by Logistics. Service installs the product, and it repairs it if the customer has a problem with it. A community focused on a specific product which includes members from all of these functions can help them collaborate across boundaries. One of the following collaboration conditions typically exists in an organisation. These are listed in increasing level of connectedness.

- There are no communities. Small work teams collaborate, but there is limited collaboration beyond the teams.
- There are some communities within functions. For example, a community of engineers who help each other out with designs.
- There are some communities which span some functions. For example, a community for engineers and service people for a specific product.
- There are some communities which span all functions. For example, a community with everyone involved in some way on a specific product.

- There are communities for all offerings which span all functions, and include customers and partners. This is true boundary spanning.

In the Implementation Plan, identify all groups which need to connect, and include boundary spanning as a required knowledge flow. The higher the level of connectedness you can achieve, the more knowledge will flow between groups. You can use social network analysis (see Chapter 8) to help determine the current state of social networks and to identify boundary spanning opportunities.

Discovery: processes for learning from existing sources of information, including systems, databases, and libraries
In most organisations there are information systems, transaction processing applications, and databases which are used to run the business. There is data captured in these systems which can be used to distill trends, answer queries, and support decision-making. And this can be done without the need to capture data redundantly. For example, if customer purchase information is entered into the order processing system, it can be fed to a data warehouse for use by all departments.

Many organisations have libraries of information obtained through outside sources. These may include competitive intelligence, analyst reports, industry news, and benchmark data. Providing access to this information supports analysis, strategy formulation, and planning. If such libraries do not exist centrally, you should consider providing them to prevent individual departments from purchasing information on their own. If they do exist, then your plan should incorporate them into the resources provided through the user interface.

Creation: processes for stimulating innovation and facilitating invention
Creating new knowledge is an important goal for most organisations, but it is difficult to enable. By using the other modes of knowledge flow – collection, connection, boundary spanning, and discovery – and adding explicit processes to use these flows to create knowledge, innovation can be stimulated.

Let's take an example. In a consulting firm, information about customer projects is captured in a repository (*collection*). Communities for each type of consulting service are active (*connection*), and include consultants, partners, contractors, and sales people from all regions of the world (*boundary spanning*). Details on the win rate, delivery time, and profitability of each service offering are available in a data warehouse (*discovery*). Competitive and industry trends are available in a corporate library (*discovery*).

The leadership team has been asked to increase the gross profit margin of the consulting business. They take the following steps.

- Search the project repository to see which customers are doing the most repeat business. Survey those customers about their upcoming needs.
- Ask the communities for each service offering to offer their suggestions for improving profits. Select the best ones for implementation.
- Analyse the information in the data warehouse to see which service offerings are the most and least profitable. Improve on the profitable ones and develop new offerings with similar attributes. Discontinue the unprofitable ones and deny approval to future proposals for offerings with similar attributes.

■ Review competitive and industry trends to see which competitors' offerings are the most profitable and what the analysts predict will be profitable. Use these findings to help shape new development efforts.

Combining all of these inputs, the leaders decide to drop their three worst-performing service offerings, invest in further developing their top three, and decide to create two new offerings based on customer input, community feedback, and analyst predictions. By institutionalising the process used in this case, a knowledge creation process can be reused for future innovation. It is not simple or intuitive to create new knowledge, but it is worth perfecting because the potential benefits are significant.

Examples of knowledge flow
Demand-driven knowledge sharing, which can also be called just-in-time knowledge management, emphasises connection instead of collection. It assumes that knowledge will be provided at the time of need.

Here is how it works. Someone has a question, problem, or need to know who, what, when, where, why, and/or how about a topic. They search existing repositories and threaded discussion archives to see if there is an existing answer. If so, they use it. If no answer is found, they post their question, problem, or need to one or more relevant threaded discussions. Other members of the threaded discussion respond with their answers. The answers may include links to content in other repositories. The answers are automatically archived so that future searches will produce useful results.

Tacit knowledge can be shared through connection, and it can be turned into explicit knowledge through collection. Communities and social networks are the usual mechanisms for sharing tacit knowledge.

Here is an example. Someone wants to share an insight, a nugget of knowledge, or a solution to a problem which others may face. They post to a relevant threaded discussion. They may choose to write up their knowledge more formally, thus turning it into explicit knowledge.

Explicit knowledge is captured through collection and shared through connection. Repositories are typically used to capture this form of knowledge.

For example, someone wants to share reusable content such as a document, presentation, recording, process, procedure, template, tool, software source code module, or some other form of data. They upload the file containing the content to the appropriate repository. They post to the related threaded discussion to let the members know about the file, including a link to it.

By considering all five modes of knowledge flow, and incorporating them appropriately into your plans, you can decide how to enable and support all needed flows. This will be incorporated in the corresponding people, process, and technology elements which you design as part of the programme. Encouraging demand-driven knowledge sharing can help knowledge flow in very practical ways.

Select and implement people, process, and technology components

Knowledge management helps people learn, share, reuse, collaborate, and innovate through people, process, and technology components. It is important to maintain a balance between people, process, and technology as you implement a KM programme.

From the Top 50 KM Components listed below, select the ones which you will use as part of your KM Strategy. Use the results of your user survey to help select the right ones. Subsequent chapters provide details on all 50 components.

People components

Culture and values: the way things are done in an organisation, and what things are considered to be important and taboo.

Knowledge managers: people who spend all or a significant portion of their time leading KM initiatives, sharing knowledge, and supporting others in sharing their knowledge.

User surveys and employee satisfaction surveys: periodic surveys to determine user preferences, needs, and challenges and to determine how employees view a KM programme and its components.

Social networks: collections of people who are acquainted or connected as friends, business contacts, or colleagues and communicate, collaborate, or help one another as needed.

Communities: groups of people who share a concern, a set of problems, or a passion about a topic, and deepen their understanding and knowledge of this area by interacting on an ongoing basis (from Etienne Wenger, Richard McDermott, and William Snyder).

Training: classroom courses, self-paced courses, and recorded webinars which allow users to learn what is expected of them; the people, processes, and tools which are available to them; and how to use all of these in order to learn, share, reuse, collaborate, and innovate.

Documentation: user guides, manuals, and help files which allow users to read about what is expected of them; the people, processes, and tools which are available to them; and how to use all of these in order to learn, share, reuse, collaborate, and innovate.

Communications: vehicles for informing current and potential users about progress in the KM initiative through websites, team spaces, portals, wikis, forums, conference calls, blogs, newsletters, distribution lists, and links.

User assistance and knowledge help desk: people who provide support by phone or e-mail to users, including tool consulting, finding reusable content, connecting to knowledge sources, process support, training, communication, and other assistance.

Goals and measurements: employee goals included in performance plans, and measurements to track performance against those goals and other operational indicators.

Incentives and rewards: programmes designed to encourage compliance with goals, improve performance against metrics, and increase participation in KM initiatives – includes tangible rewards, recognition, and competitive rankings.

Process components

Methodologies: policies, rules, techniques, and procedures which prescribe how work is to be performed and provide proven ways to do it successfully.

Creation: inventing new concepts, approaches, methods, techniques, products, services, and ideas which can be used for the benefit of people and organisations.

Capture: collecting documents, presentations, spreadsheets, records, processes, software source, images, audio, video, and other files which can be used for learning, reuse, and innovation.

Reuse: putting to practical use the captured knowledge, community suggestions, and collaborative assistance provided through knowledge sharing.

Lessons learnt: explaining what an individual or team has learnt as a result of their experience, using documents, presentations, discussions, and recordings – including what they tried, what worked, what didn't work, what to do, what to avoid, problems faced, how problems were solved, what they would do differently, and key insights and nuggets.

Proven practices: selecting, documenting, and replicating processes which have proven to improve business results so that others in similar environments or with similar needs can benefit from the proven successes.

Collaboration: interacting with peers and colleagues to exchange ideas, share experiences, work together on projects, and solve problems.

Content management: creating, managing, distributing, publishing, and retrieving structured information – the complete lifecycle of content as it moves through an organisation.

Classification: creating and maintaining a taxonomy that can be used to organise information so that it can be readily found through navigation, search, and links between related content.

Metrics and reporting: capturing operational indicators and producing reports to communicate performance against goals, areas for improvement, and progress toward the desired state.

Management of change: developing a planned approach to change in an organisation to address anticipated obstacles and to ensure successful adoption.

Workflow: embedding knowledge creation, capture, and reuse in business processes so that these steps happen routinely as part of normal work.

Valuation: quantifying the value of reuse and innovation so that it can be fully appreciated by the organisation, including customer pricing, cost benefit analysis, and project justification.

Social network analysis: mapping and measuring of relationships and flows between people, groups, organisations, animals, computers or other information/knowledge processing entities; the nodes in the network are the people and groups while the links show relationships or flows between the nodes – provides both a visual and a mathematical analysis of human relationships (from Valdis Krebs).

Appreciative inquiry: asking questions that strengthen a system's capacity to apprehend, anticipate, and heighten positive potential – mobilisation of inquiry through the crafting of the "unconditional positive question".

Storytelling: using narrative to ignite action, implement new ideas, communicate who you are, build your brand, instill organisational values, foster collaboration to get things done, share knowledge, neutralise gossip and rumour, and lead people into the future (from Steve Denning).

Technology components

User interface: the point of entry to a knowledge base that provides navigation, search, communication, help, news, site index, site map, and links to all tools.

Intranet: a private computer network that uses Internet protocols, network connectivity, and possibly the public telecommunication system to securely share part of an organisation's information or operations with its employees (from Wikipedia).

Team spaces: collaborative workspaces designed to allow teams to share documents, libraries, schedules, and files; conduct meetings, calls, surveys, and polls; and store meeting minutes, discussions, reports, and plans.

Virtual meeting rooms: online, real-time tools designed to allow teams to share presentations, applications, and white boards during meetings.

Portals: websites that provide personalised capabilities to users through the use of customisation, building blocks, and integration of multiple sources.

Repositories: structured lists and databases which allow documents and other files to be stored, searched for, and retrieved.

Bulletin boards and threaded discussions: forums for carrying on discussions among subscribers on a specific subject, including online and e-mail posts and replies, searchable archives, and discussions grouped by threads to show the complete history on each topic.

Expertise locators and ask the expert: systems for finding experts on particular subjects, allowing individuals to enter details about what they know and can do, and others to search for all people having desired skills, experience, or knowledge; and systems for asking questions of experts and getting the answers.

Metadata and tags: information about information – data fields added to documents, websites, files, or lists which allow related items to be listed, searched for, navigated to, syndicated, and collected.

Search engines: tools which allow searching for documents, files, list items, content, and answers to questions – allow for specifying the scope or domain of the search, whether to search on text or metadata, and how results should be presented.

Archiving: offline file storage for legal, audit, or historical purposes, using tapes, CDs, or other long-term media.

Blogs: websites where entries are made (such as in a journal or diary), displayed in a reverse chronological order; often provide commentary or news on a particular subject; some function as personal online diaries or logbooks; combine text, images, and links to other blogs and websites; typically provide archives in calendar form, local search, syndication feeds, reader comment posting, trackback links from other blogs, blogroll links to other recommended blogs, and categories of entries tagged for retrieval by topic.

Wikis: websites which allow users to easily add, remove, edit, and change most available content – effective for collaborative writing and self-service website creation and maintenance.

Podcasts: recorded broadcasts which can be listened to online, or downloaded manually or automatically through syndication and then listened to on portable MP3 players at the listener's convenience.

Syndication and aggregation: using feeds available from a website to provide an updated list of its content in the form of a subscription, an embedded portion of a website, or a collection of disparate content on a particular topic – typically uses RSS or Atom syndication and .rss, .xml, or .rdf files for the feeds.

Social software: a range of tools which facilitate social networking, typically personal web pages including bios, photos, interests, audio and video, links to friends, messages from friends, and personal networks; often referred to as Web 2.0 to include a broad range of tools such as blogs, wikis, and RSS feeds.

External access: capability for users outside of a company's firewall to have access to selected websites and team spaces to allow collaboration with retirees, partners, and customers who would otherwise be blocked from the company's internal network – requires technical, security, and legal elements.

Workflow applications: software which connects and sequences different applications, components, and people, all of which must be involved in the processing of data to complete an instance of a process.

Process automation applications: tools which automate previously manual processes, such as the production of proposals, creation of presentations, or the design of products.

E-learning: tools which enable the delivery and tracking of online training courses.

Subscription management: tools which allow content providers to reach subscribers on an opt-in basis, and subscribers to sign up to receive periodicals and other communications based on their interests.

Incentive points tracking: systems for awarding and tracking points for desired KM behaviours, both automatically as triggered by events and manually through forms entry.

Survey and metrics reporting automation: systems for conducting, collecting, and publishing survey data; and systems for collecting, distributing, and publishing data on key performance metrics.

Summary

Publish and maintain on an easily-accessible website the Implementation Plan, including programme governance, knowledge flows, overall implementation schedule, overall new release schedule, and detailed plans and schedules for all selected people, process, and technology components.
The Implementation Plan ensures that the KM programme is put into action in order to achieve the Top Three Objectives previously identified.

Chapter 7: People components

This chapter examines the principal people components of the Top 50 KM Components outlined in Chapter 6.

- Culture and values.
- Knowledge managers.
- User surveys and employee satisfaction surveys.
- Social networks.
- Communities.
- Training.
- Documentation.
- Communications.
- User assistance and knowledge help desk.
- Goals and measurements.
- Incentives and rewards.

A discussion of each component is provided, along with links for additional information.

Culture and values

The way things are done in an organisation, and what things are considered to be important and taboo.

Chapter 5 discussed the culture and values of your organisation and creating a culture dominated by positive elements. A knowledge sharing culture includes three elements:

- Knowledge reuse is valued over reinvention.
- Sharing knowledge helps you advance in your career.
- In the process of innovating, failure is encouraged – as long as the lessons learnt are shared so that similar failures are prevented.

To help instil a knowledge sharing culture, create a vision of how things should work in the organisation. Specify how learning, sharing, reusing, collaborating, and innovating should be done. Have the senior executive and the leadership team communicate the vision widely and regularly. Here is an example of people, process, and technology elements in a vision for a knowledge sharing culture.

People

- Managers regularly inspect, talk about, and directly participate in knowledge sharing and reuse.
- All employees belong to and regularly participate in at least one community.
- Desired knowledge behaviours are rewarded significantly, regularly, consistently, and visibly.
- Time is allowed for knowledge management tasks.
- Employee promotions require demonstrated knowledge sharing, and everyone knows this.

Process

- All project teams reuse standard, institutionalised knowledge from previous, similar projects.
- All project teams submit reusable content to the appropriate repositories at standard milestones.
- Knowledge management processes are integrated with standard business processes in a way that is transparent to users.
- Proven practices are replicated.

- All reusable content is checked for quality, scrubbed to remove confidential data, and provided in standard formats.

Technology

- It is easy for any question to be asked or any problem to be posed such that a useful answer or solution is provided rapidly, regardless of the location of the requestor, the time of day, or the nature of the request.
- Useful information is delivered to users when they need it based on the work that they are doing.
- Information flows are automated between all systems and tools so that no data needs to be re-entered.
- Users can access the knowledge they need even if they are not connected to the network.
- All teams collaborate using team spaces.

Encouraging people to share knowledge
To change from a culture of knowledge hoarding to one of knowledge sharing, examine why people may not be sharing their knowledge with one another.
Here are the main reasons, along with recommended solutions, using reasons from *Why Employees Don't Do What They're Supposed To Do and What To Do About It* by Ferdinand Fournies at http://www.amazon.com/gp/product/0071342559/.

They don't have time. They think they have no time for knowledge sharing. Solution: embed knowledge-sharing into the basic work and processes of your organisation so that it is not viewed as a separate task which can be avoided.

They don't trust others. They are worried that sharing their knowledge will allow other people to be rewarded without giving credit or something in return, or result in the misuse of that knowledge. Solution: reward people on team goals, and nurture communities within the organisation to create an environment of trust.

They think that knowledge is power. They hoard their knowledge waiting for someone to beg them for it, treat them like a guru, or give them something in return. Solution: recognise, reward, and promote those who share their knowledge, while denying promotions to those who fail to do so.

They don't know why they should do it. They don't think they need to spend time on knowledge sharing. Leadership has not made a strong case for knowledge sharing. Solution: set specific knowledge-sharing goals for employees and communicate them repeatedly through many different channels. Have the senior executive communicate regularly on knowledge sharing expectations, goals, and rewards.

They don't know how to do it. They are unclear about how and where to share their knowledge. They have not received training and communications on how to share knowledge. Solution: develop, deliver, and make available on-demand training which makes it clear how to share knowledge, including links to the relevant tools and systems. Regularly communicate and conduct webinars and knowledge fairs. Web-based training should be available for all tools.

They don't know what they are supposed to do. Leadership has not established and communicated clear goals for knowledge sharing. Solution: establish and communicate clear knowledge-sharing goals.

They think the recommended way will not work. They have received training and communications but don't believe what they are being asked to do will work. Solution: the KM leaders, knowledge assistants, and other members of the KM team have to convince people in small groups or in one-on-one sessions by showing them that it does work.

They think their way is better. They are used to working on their own or collaborating only with a small group of trusted comrades and believe this is the best way. Solution: regularly share stories of how others are benefitting from sharing knowledge using the recommended ways. This should help sway those stuck in their current ways to consider using better ways.

They think something else is more important. They believe that there are higher-priority tasks than knowledge sharing. Solution: get all first-level managers to model knowledge-sharing behaviour for their employees, and to inspect compliance to knowledge-sharing goals with the same fervour as they inspect other goals.

There is no positive consequence to them for doing it. They receive no rewards, recognition, promotions, or other benefits for sharing knowledge. Solution: implement rewards and recognition programmes for those who share their knowledge. For example, award points to those who share knowledge, and then give desirable rewards to those with the top point totals.

They think they are doing it. They are sharing knowledge differently than the recommended ways (e.g., sending e-mail to trusted colleagues or distribution lists). Solution: assign people to work with each

community and organisation to show them how to use the recommended ways and how they work better than other ways. Providing a new tool or process which is viewed as a killer application – it quickly and widely catches on – is the best way for the old ways to be replaced with new ways.

They are rewarded for not doing it. They hoard their knowledge and thus get people to beg for their help, or they receive rewards, recognition, or promotions based on doing other tasks. Solution: work with all managers in the organisation to encourage them to reinforce the desired behaviours and stop rewarding the wrong behaviours.

They are punished for doing it. As a result of spending time on knowledge sharing, they don't achieve other goals which are more important to the organisation. Solution: align knowledge-sharing processes and goals with other critical processes and performance goals.

They anticipate a negative consequence for doing it. They are afraid that if they share knowledge, they will lose their status as a guru (no one will have to come begging to them at the time of need), or that they will not achieve other more important goals. Solution: position knowledge sharing as being a critical success factor for the organisation.

There is no negative consequence to them for not doing it. Knowledge sharing is not one of their performance goals, or it is a goal which is not enforced. Solution: work with all first-level managers to get them to implement, inspect, and enforce knowledge-sharing goals. This needs to come from the top – if the leader senior executive insists on it and checks up on compliance, it will happen.

There are obstacles beyond their control. They are not allowed to spend time sharing knowledge, they don't have access to systems for knowledge sharing, or they don't have strong English language skills for sharing with those outside of their country. Solutions: embed knowledge sharing into normal business processes. Provide ways to collaborate when not connected (e.g., using e-mail for threaded discussions). Encourage those with weak English skills to share within their countries in their native languages.

Creating culture and instilling values
Creating a knowledge sharing culture and instilling positive values to enable the required people, process, and technology elements are critical success factors for any KM initiative. You can use the ten other people components described below to understand and influence corporate culture.

Employee surveys can determine prevailing attitudes. Social networks can spread the key messages and reinforce the core values. Communities can be asked for advice on improving the culture, used for change management, and created to introduce new processes such as appreciative inquiry. Training is necessary to communicate values and standards. Documentation should spell out expectations for employees. Regular communications from leaders about vision, mission, strategy should refer to relevant training and documentation. Goals and measurements should reflect the desired culture. Incentives and rewards should support the official values.

In *Common knowledge: how companies thrive by sharing what they know* at http://harvardbusinessonline.hbsp.harvard.edu/b01/en/common/viewFileNavBean.jhtml?_requestid=38818, Nancy Dixon writes:

"The third myth… is that the exchange of knowledge happens only in organisations that have a noncompetitive or a collaborative culture. It follows that the first thing you have to do is to fix the culture and then get people to share. But I have found that it's the other way around. If people begin sharing ideas about issues they see as really important, the sharing itself creates a learning culture."

Resources on culture and values

'Five reasons people don't tell what they know' by Carol Kinsey Goman at http://destinationkm.com/articles/default.asp?ArticleID=960

'Overcoming cultural barriers to sharing knowledge' by Richard McDermott and Carla O'Dell at http://www.knowledgeboard.com/lib/3467

'European Guide to good Practice in Knowledge Management - Part 2: Organizational Culture' at ftp://cenftp1.cenorm.be/PUBLIC/CWAs/e-Europe/KM/CWA14924-02-2004-Mar.pdf

'Creating a knowledge-sharing culture' at http://engage.comms.gov.uk/knowledge-bank/internal-communication/successful-internal-communication/5-creating-a-knowledge-sharing-culture.html

'Organizational Culture' by Carter McNamara at http://www.managementhelp.org/org_thry/culture/culture.htm

'Love Is the Killer App' by Tim Sanders at http://www.fastcompany.com/magazine/55/love.html

'On Trust and Culture' by Karen Otazo at http://www.strategy-business.com/press/article/06311

'Understanding Corporate Culture' by Tim Bryce at http://managementvisions.blogspot.com/2006/10/october-9-2006.html

'The Wealth of Knowledge: Intellectual Capital and the Twenty-first Century Organization' (http://www.amazon.com/gp/product/0385500726/) by Thomas Stewart, Chapter 11 "A New Culture: Developing at Knowledge Perspective"

Knowledge managers

People who spend all or a significant portion of their time leading KM initiatives, sharing knowledge, and supporting others in sharing their knowledge.

You will need to have at least one knowledge manager to lead the KM initiative. Knowledge management is everyone's responsibility, not just the work of knowledge managers. But knowledge managers are needed to raise awareness, align knowledge actions with business priorities, promote a knowledge sharing culture, engage senior leadership, manage the infrastructure, and support all knowledge workers.

Good knowledge managers are part connector, part maven, and part salesman, to use Malcolm Gladwell's terms from *The Tipping Point* (http://www.amazon.com/gp/product/0316346624/). From 'Visualizing The Tipping Point' by David Armano at http://darmano.typepad.com/logic_emotion/2006/07/visualizing_the.html:

"Connectors are those with wide social circles. They are the hubs of the human social network and are responsible for the small world phenomenon. They connect people to each other.

Mavens are knowledgeable people. While most consumers wouldn't know if a product were priced above the market rate by, say, 10%, mavens would. Bloggers who detect false claims in the media could also be considered mavens. They help people through sharing knowledge.

Salesmen are charismatic people with powerful negotiation skills. They exert soft influence rather than forceful power. Their source of influence may be the tendency of others, subconsciously, to imitate them rather than techniques of conscious persuasion. They use knowledge to engage and persuade."

Knowledge managers know how to use KM tools, how to ask others for help, who should be connected to whom, who would benefit from a piece of information, and how to persuade others to use information effectively. One role of a knowledge manager is subscribing to many information sources, belonging to many communities, and reading many publications, always looking out for what may be useful to others in the organisation.

All good managers should do these things, but they may not know how to best do so. A KM programme can support managers in all of these activities. Good knowledge managers regularly inform their management colleagues about an article, book, presentation, or con call which was relevant to their areas of responsibility. These colleagues can subscribe to the same sources and join the same communities, but if not, they will appreciate being selectively alerted when content applies to them.

All knowledge workers in the organisation should view learning, sharing, reuse, collaboration, and innovation to be part of their jobs. But as Malcolm Gladwell wrote, not everyone is a connector, maven, or salesman. So those who play these roles, and especially, those who combine more than one of these roles, can function as power knowledge workers, facilitating knowledge flow throughout the organisation.

According to Peter West of Continuous Innovation (http://www.continuousinnovation.ca/AboutUs.html):

"The differentiator rests with the organisation-wide awareness-raising, focus, passion and leadership that a knowledge manager can instill. The concern that many have with the formal identification of a knowledge manager (or a chief knowledge officer) is that it may inadvertently convey the message that knowledge processes and, more importantly, knowledge responsibilities have been centralised. Unfortunately, some knowledge managers become knowledge bottlenecks instead of knowledge conduits."

Good knowledge managers have worked in many different roles so that they have experienced first-hand the needs of employees. They know about the organisation, including who does what, where to find information, and the ways things get done. Within the organisation, they are active in communities, subscribe to newsletters, attend seminars and conference calls, and visit websites. Outside, they attend seminars and conferences, read books, subscribe to periodicals, visit blogs and websites, and participate in online communities.

Knowledge managers look for knowledge-related needs that are not currently met, and try to develop ways to meet these needs using people, process, or technology. They like to help others who are looking for information, trying to figure out how to use tools, or seeking others. They introduce people to one another, invite them to join communities, and pass along items of interest which they encounter. Knowledge

managers fill the roles of KM leaders, project leaders, and knowledge assistants (see Chapter 6). Here is the profile of a good knowledge manager.

Knowledge manager profile

Experience

- Management: supervised people, led work teams, managed a business or functional unit.
- Project management: successfully managed projects to meet deadlines, provide deliverables, and adhered to budgets.
- Communications: published documents, gave presentations, and managed communications programmes.
- Top 50 KM Components: for many of these, performed evaluations, led implementation projects, and used them regularly.
- Reputation: has earned the respect of people both inside and outside of the organisation based on accomplishments, networking, and communications.

Skills

- Leadership: able to influence others, lead work teams, and manage projects.
- Communications: excellent at writing, speaking, presenting, and using a variety of communications vehicles.
- Process and technology: able to quickly learn and master a wide variety of tools and processes.
- Top 50 KM Components: expert at using many of these.
- Analysis: able to seek input, analyse information, consider alternatives, and make good decisions.

Attributes

- Adaptable
  - Flexible: willing to try different courses of action.
  - Resilient: overcomes difficulties, withstands setbacks, and meets challenges.
  - Open-minded: considers the opinions of others.

- Assertive
  - Takes initiative.
  - Consistently achieves challenging objectives and meets commitments.
  - Makes effective decisions in a timely manner.

- Calm
  - Maintains a high level of performance even when under pressure.
  - Even-tempered even when dealing with unpleasant circumstances.
  - Balances logic and emotions when interacting with others.

- Client-focused
  - Understands clients' needs and concerns.
  - Responds promptly and effectively to client needs.
  - Eager to be of help to users.

- Creative
  - Develops innovative approaches to problem solving.
  - Invents new ways of doing things.
  - Willing to try out bold ideas.

- Collaborative
  - Acknowledges others' contributions.
  - Works effectively with individuals of different backgrounds and from different groups.
  - Willing to seek help as needed.
  - Shares personal knowledge.
  - Builds partnerships and networks.

- Curious
  - Stays current in the field.
  - Open to new ideas.
  - Asks others to share their knowledge and experience.

- Dynamic
  - Gets results.
  - Balances analysis with action.
  - Sets high standards.

- Influential
  - Gains support and commitment from others even without formal authority.
  - Resolves differences by determining needs and forging solutions that benefit all parties.
  - Facilitates teamwork across organisational boundaries.

- Personable
  - Gets along well with many different types of people.
  - Nurtures new relationships.
  - Well-liked as a manager, employee, and colleague.

For more information on knowledge managers, see 'Knowledge Managers: Who They Are and What They Do' by James D. McKeen and D. Sandy Staples at http://www.providersedge.com/docs/km_articles/Knowledge_Managers_-_Who_They_Are_and_What_They_Do.pdf

User surveys and employee satisfaction surveys

Periodic surveys to determine user preferences, needs, and challenges and to determine how employees view a KM programme and its components

Surveys are essential at the start of a KM initiative to ensure that the programme meets the needs of the organisation. You should also develop processes for soliciting ongoing suggestions, providing feedback, and submitting change requests. There are three different types of surveys you can conduct to help ensure that your programme meets the needs of your users.

Use an *Opportunities Survey* to identify current challenges and needs, and request suggestions for addressing them. Use this survey to determine business needs which knowledge management can support. This survey is generally conducted once when starting a new KM initiative, but can be used periodically to ensure that new requirements are identified.

Conduct a *Resource Survey* to compile a list of people, process, and technology components which are currently in use, determine the usefulness of each one, and request suggestions for additions. Use this survey to find out which tools are currently popular and to identify gaps in meeting user needs. This survey is generally conducted at the beginning of a KM programme, and periodically repeated to calibrate and adjust the programme components.

Implement a regular *Employee Satisfaction Survey* to solicit feedback on how your KM programme is perceived by its users. Use this survey to stay in touch with how your users view the programme, what they like, and what needs to be improved. This survey should be conducted monthly during the first year of a KM initiative, and annually thereafter if the results remain fairly stable.

How to conduct surveys
Surveys can be conducted in three ways. It is best to choose one method and stick with it to provide a consistent user experience.

Online surveys are delivered on a website which recipients must visit. E-mail surveys are sent to participants and must be returned. Personal surveys are conducted on a one-to-one basis.

Online surveys are generally quick and easy for users to complete. Your organisation may have developed or purchased its own internal survey tool. If such a tool is available, use it. If not, you can create a custom web form using a web page editor, a team space tool, or by reusing one from another source. You can also create a custom word processing document which can be delivered on a web page, filled in, and sent by e-mail.

Publicly-available services such as Zoomerang at http://info.zoomerang. com/ and SurveyMonkey at http://www. surveymonkey.com/ offer both paid and free services. Zoomerang Basic is limited to 100 or fewer participants and 30 or fewer questions, and results expire after ten days. Ongoing membership is free. SurveyMonkey's basic subscription is totally free and includes all of the basic features of SurveyMonkey. Basic subscribers are limited to a total of ten questions and 100 responses per survey. They offer a comparison with other online services at http://www.surveymonkey. com/Pricing.asp.

E-mail surveys are sent as a message with a simple form to be completed and returned. Take care to design the form to be easy to complete and easy to compile the results. Use tick boxes and radio buttons as much as possible, using free text entry only when necessary for open-ended questions.

People Components

Personal surveys involve asking the respondents to answer a few questions during a telephone conversation or in person. The person conducting the survey should enter the results directly into a form or document so that they are captured electronically. The advantage of this type of survey is that the questions can be open-ended, customised, and tailored based on the answers being provided. If the conversation heads in a particular direction, the interviewer can adjust dynamically.

Of these three types, the online survey is generally the best, since the data is automatically collected and reports can be immediately produced. E-mail surveys are inexpensive and easy to create and useful if they are primarily requests for open-ended text responses. Personal surveys are useful for small sample sizes when you wish to directly hear from the respondents and learn from the conversations.

How to distribute surveys
You can distribute your survey in one of three ways. A wide distribution is good for capturing inputs from an entire population, although not everyone will participate. A representative sample works well when the population is large and it would be costly or disruptive to include everyone. And a targeted subset should be used if you want to get feedback from a special class of respondents.

To solicit inputs from everyone in the organisation, send an e-mail message to a wide distribution list. For an online survey, include a link to the survey website. For an e-mail survey, include the actual survey, either in the body of the message or as an attachment. For a personal survey, include a request for a phone or in-person appointment. Be prepared to receive replies from only a small percentage of

the population. If you want to increase the response rate, have the senior executive send the message, with follow-up messages once or twice after the initial distribution.

For a random subset of the organisation, send a message to a representative sample of your target audience. Select a random cross-section of the total population that should include a wide range of typical users. Strive for a balance in the geographic and organisational composition of the sample. For recurring surveys, ensure that once surveyed, participants are not surveyed again for at least one year. This will ensure the ongoing diversity of replies, and avoid pestering recipients with repeated requests.

If you want to reach a specific class of user, send the message to a targeted subset of people who meet selected criteria. For example, you may wish to reach those who perform a specialised role particularly relevant to the survey. Or you may wish to determine the views of people who are highly respected throughout the organisation and follow their suggestions. It may also be useful to poll thought leaders since they will influence many others in the organisation.

The e-mail message should be concise and explain why the survey is being conducted; why it is important to them; what will be done with their input; how long it will take to complete; and how to complete it, or for a personal survey, how to schedule an appointment or when someone will follow up to do so.

To increase the response rate, you might wish to use one of the following tactics. Offer an inexpensive prize (e.g., a mouse pad) to the first 50 people who reply. Give an expensive prize (e.g., an MP3 player or a personal digital assistant) to someone chosen at random or to the most complete or helpful reply. Have the senior executive send out the survey with a personal plea or mandate for participation. For a survey sent to targeted audience, inform the recipients that they were specially selected because they are highly respected thought leaders whose opinions are valued. Set a deadline for replies that is long enough to allow people to catch up or return from vacation. But make the time allowed short enough so that recipients know that they have a limited time only to participate. Two or three weeks is a typical amount of time to allow.

Opportunities survey

Use this survey when you are creating your Top Three Objectives List. It allows you to test your assumptions and ensure that your programme is designed to meet the needs of your organisation. This should be conducted once before beginning any new KM initiative.

Here is an example of a survey you can use. You can adapt this as necessary to your situation.

Opportunities survey

Tick all of the following challenges you are currently experiencing.

☐ It's difficult for my team to make decisions, and when we make them, they are bad.

☐ It's hard to find relevant information and resources at the time of need.

☐ We have to start from scratch each time we start a new project, and my team keeps reinventing the wheel.

☐ We repeat the same mistakes over and over.

☐ It's difficult to find out if anyone else has solved a similar problem before or already done similar work.

☐ Information is poorly communicated to me, and I am unaware of what has been done, what is happening, and where the organisation is heading.

☐ I can't find standard processes, procedures, methods, tools, templates, techniques, and examples.

☐ I can't get experts to help me, because they are scarce, in great demand, and unavailable when needed.

☐ We are unable to respond to customers who ask for proof that we know how to help them and that we have done similar work before.

☐ It takes too long to invent, design, manufacture, sell, and deliver products and services to our customers.

List any other challenges you regularly experience with learning, sharing, reusing, collaborating, innovating, and searching for knowledge.

....
....
....
....
....
....
....
....
....
....
....
....
....
....
....

From the challenges which you ticked and the ones you listed, please rank the three most important in decreasing order of importance:

<fill in the most important challenge>
<fill in the second most important challenge>
<fill in the third most important challenge>

What examples can you provide where learning, sharing, reusing, collaborating, innovating, and searching for knowledge are working well today?

....
....
....
....
....
....
....
....
....
....

What examples can you provide where learning, sharing, reusing, collaborating, innovating, and searching for knowledge worked well in the past?

....
....
....
....
....
....
....
....
....
....

What examples can you provide where learning, sharing, reusing, collaborating, innovating, and searching for knowledge worked well in the past or are working well today in other organisations?

....
....
....
....
....

....
....
....
....
....

What suggestions do you have for dealing with any of the challenges you identified?

....
....
....
....
....
....
....
....
....
....
....

What other needs do you have for learning, sharing, reusing, collaborating, innovating, and searching for knowledge?

....
....
....
....
....
....
....
....
....
....

What suggestions do you have for meeting the needs you identified?

....
....
....
....

....
....
....
....
....

Describe how KM would work ideally.

....
....
....
....
....
....
....
....

Resource survey
Use this survey to evaluate existing knowledge resources and to determine which ones to add. It allows you to learn which resources are worthwhile, which ones are not, which ones you should learn more about, and which ones should be added. This should be conducted once when starting a KM initiative to help select the KM components to use, and every one to three years thereafter to make adjustments to the ones selected. Here is an example of a survey you can use.

Demographic questions

What is your e-mail address?

....

What is your location?

....

What is your organisation, including group and sub-group?

....

What is your job role?

....

How many years have you worked in the organisation?

....

Multiple choice questions

For each of the following knowledge resource websites, please answer the first question. If the answer is 'Yes', please also answer the second question.

[You, the compiler of the survey, will need to provide a complete list of knowledge resources currently available in your organisation. Use the Top 50 KM Components from the introduction to help identify and categorise the resources. List those resources identified here in the survey.]

In the last 30 days, have you used this website?

☐ Yes
☐ No
☐ Don't know

If you have used the site in the last 30 days, how useful is this website to you in your work?

☐ Very useful
☐ Moderately useful
☐ Not useful
☐ Don't know

Open-ended questions

Are there other valuable knowledge resources you use frequently? If so, what are they?

....
....
....
....
....

....

....

....

....

When you need to find knowledge to help you learn, where do you go first?

....

....

....

....

When you want to share your knowledge, where do you go first?

....

....

....

....

When you need to find knowledge to reuse, where do you go first?

....

....

....

....

When you want to collaborate with colleagues, where do you go first?

....

....

....

....

When you need to find knowledge to help you innovate, where do you go first?

Do you have comments about any of the knowledge resources mentioned in the survey?

....

....

....

What knowledge resources would you like to see added or created?

....

....

....

Are there knowledge resources you would like to see improved? If so, how?

....

....

....

What knowledge resources do you think you need to access but don't currently have access to?

....

....

....

....

Employee satisfaction survey
Use this survey on an ongoing basis to set a baseline and measure progress. It allows you to learn how your users view your programme, what is perceived as working

well, and what you need to improve. This should be conducted with a representative sample of the population on a monthly basis after the start of a KM initiative. If the results reach a fairly stable level, then the frequency can be reduced to once a year. Include the results in your regular programme metrics reporting. Here is an example of a survey you can use. You can adapt this as necessary to your situation.

Employee satisfaction survey

How satisfied are you with your manager's support for you spending time on knowledge sharing and reuse?

....
....

How satisfied are you with your ability to access knowledge resources when you are not connected to the network?

....
....

How satisfied are you with the ability of knowledge reuse activities to save time and/or effort in your work?

....
....

How satisfied are you with your ability to find the information and knowledge you need to do your job?

....
....
....

How satisfied are you with the system availability of the online knowledge resources you use most often?

....
....
....

How satisfied are you with the experience of searching repositories to find reusable content?

....
....

How satisfied are you with the experience of locating an expert?

....
....

How satisfied are you with the ease of collaborating with internal colleagues?

....
....
....

How satisfied are you with the ease of collaborating with customers, partners, and external colleagues?

....
....

How satisfied are you with your ability to join, participate, and derive value from communities of practice?

....
....

How satisfied are you with training and documentation for using knowledge resources?

....
....

How satisfied are you with the services provided by the knowledge help desk?

....
....
....

Do you have a success story you can share with using the knowledge resources?

....
....

Finding out what your users are struggling with, what they would like to have provided, what they are using, and how they like what you are providing to them is an important part of being responsive. You should avoid appearing isolated, arrogant, or disinterested to your constituents. But realise that you will never be able to satisfy everyone, or satisfy anyone completely. Strive for continuous improvement, and ensure that people at least acknowledge that you are trying to do so.

For more information on surveys, see 'Online Survey Design Guide' from the University of Maryland's Laboratory for Automation Psychology and Decision Processes at http://lap.umd.edu/survey_design/index.html.

Social networks

Collections of people who are acquainted or connected as friends, business contacts, or colleagues and communicate, collaborate, or help one another as needed.

People establish relationships with other people for friendship, social activities, business development, and career advancement. Another important reason is to share knowledge and learn from each other in order to work more effectively. In this context, networks allow people to ask questions, offer advice and expertise, get a different perspective, act as a sounding board and sanity check, share trusted information, connect to other people and other networks, give support, receive coaching and counseling, and assist in career development through references, referrals, and hiring. There are internal an external versions of three different types of social networks which people form, join, and expand.

Internal work-related networks include peers in the same formal work teams, virtual teams, project teams, task forces, committees, and communities. These are the people with whom you regularly work in order to accomplish assigned objectives. For example, employees involved in contract administration.

External work-related networks include counterparts in different organisations who have regular business dealings. These are business partners, suppliers, subcontractors, customers, vendors, governing bodies, associations, and other entities who depend on one another. For example, sales account managers and the purchasing agents in their customer accounts.

Internal interest-related networks include colleagues throughout the organisation who share an interest in a topic and touch base periodically or through involvement in internal communities. The topic may not relate directly to the current job assignment. For example, Green Belts, Black Belts, or Master Black Belts in Six Sigma methods.

External interest-related networks include colleagues in different organisations who share an interest in a topic and touch base periodically or through involvement in external communities. These networks are often built through attendance at conferences, reading and publishing in periodicals, participation in threaded discussions, and commenting on each other's blogs. For example, those who attend a KM conference and participate in a birds-of-a-feather lunch discussion.

Internal personal networks include those who have worked together in the past, reside in the same office, or who have met at meetings or training classes and developed friendships. These people stay in touch primarily for social reasons, but they help each other whenever possible. For example, members of different groups who spent three weeks together attending the same new hire training class.

External personal networks include those who know each other socially, have worked together in the past, or who have met while traveling. These people may exchange business cards, add each other to their contact lists, and connect using social software such as LinkedIn (http://www.linkedin.com/) or openBC (http://www.openbc.com/). For example, neighbours who all work in different industries.

A KM programme should make it easy for people to discover others to add to their personal networks, offer processes for analysing social networks, and provide tools to facilitate finding, communicating, and collaborating with others. For a related process, see 'social network analysis' in the chapter on Process Components. For a related technology, see 'social software' in the chapter on Technology Components.

For more information, see:

- *Achieving Success Through Social Capital: Tapping Hidden Resources in Your Personal and Business Networks* by Wayne Baker at http://www.amazon.com/gp/product/0787953091/
- 'Personal Networking FAQ' at http://www.profnet.org/faq.html
- 'Knowledge Networking' by David Gurteen at http://www.gurteen.com/gurteen/gurteen.nsf/0/B7E3775A89264C4E80256C97003E7523/
- 'How Online Social Networks Benefit Organizations' by Lisa Kimball and Howard Rheingold at http://www.rheingold.com/Associates/onlinenetworks.html

- 'Social Networking: Still Not Meeting its Critical Promise' by Dave Pollard at http://blogs.salon.com/0002007/categories/businessInnovation/2006/08/14.html#a1612

Communities

Groups of people who share a concern, a set of problems, or a passion about a topic, and deepen their understanding and knowledge of this area by interacting on an ongoing basis (from Etienne Wenger, Richard McDermott, and William Snyder).

Communities should be part of any KM programme. Connecting people is fundamental to getting knowledge flowing, and communities are an important way of doing so. Here are three keys for a successful community of practice.

A *compelling topic*: the members and potential members must be passionate about the subject for collaboration, and it must be relevant to their work.

A *critical mass* of members: you usually need at least 50 members, with 100 being a better target.

A *committed leader*: the community leader should know the subject, have energy for stimulating collaboration, have sufficient time to devote to leadership, and then regularly spend time increasing membership, lining up speakers, hosting calls and meetings, asking and answering questions, and posting information which is useful to the members.

Since communities are so important, they have their own chapter in this report. Chapter 10 discusses communities in depth.

For more information on communities, see 'Communities of practice: a brief introduction' by Etienne Wenger at http://www.ewenger.com/theory/.

Training

Classroom courses, self-paced courses, and recorded webinars which allow users to learn what is expected of them; the people, processes, and tools which are available to them; and how to use all of these in order to learn, share, reuse, collaborate, and innovate.

Training is required when introducing a new KM initiative, as it is rolled out across your organisation, and as a key part of ongoing implementation. You can never succeed in successfully educating everyone in your target audience, so you have to continue to offer training in a variety of ways. Develop a training plan that includes the following vehicles.

Classroom courses are the best way of obtaining the undivided attention of those to be trained, but it is often difficult to raise funds allocated for expenses and schedule student time for attendance. Webinars and self-paced courses may offer the most realistic method of delivering training.

Webinars are virtual training courses conducted using some combination of the following elements.

■ Conference call: Participants dial in by phone to listen to the instructor and to ask questions.
■ Web conferencing: Participants log into a virtual meeting room where they can view presentations, demonstrations, interactive white boards and chat with other participants.
■ Multimedia: Webcasts which broadcast video, audio, and slides and allow questions to be typed into a web form.

■ Team space: Collaborative workspace where presentations can be accessed and followed while listening on a conference call.
■ Real-time navigation to web pages: Participants visit web pages as instructed on a conference call to view systems and applications.
■ Recording: A live event can be recorded and replayed later at the convenience of the participants. Audio is recorded and the participant listens (by phone or by audio file) and follows along by visiting the team space or specified web pages. Alternatively, the virtual meeting room presentation or webcast is recorded as a multimedia file.

Self-paced courses are automated, interactive presentations which can incorporate the following elements.

■ Web pages: Students read web pages and follow along sequentially.
■ Multimedia: Flash web pages, audio, and video are used to present content dynamically.
■ Interactive questions: Students are asked questions as they take the course, and receive immediate feedback.
■ Dynamic branching: Students can choose paths based on their interests or their answers to questions.
■ Bookmarks: Students can start and stop at any time, and when they return, they can resume from where they left off.
■ Delivery method: How the course is presented to the student. Options include web-based – delivered entirely through a web browser, either on the intranet or Internet; client-based – delivered as a downloaded application run on the PC client; and portable

media-based – delivered as a CD, DVD, or flash memory plug-in.

Training plan

The training plan should include the following elements for each course.

Content: what subjects will be covered

- Introduction: a high-level overview of the KM initiative and its components.
- Survey: a more thorough overview including details on the most important components.
- In-depth topic (e.g., one of the Top 50 KM components, a particular process or tool, or a method or technique).

Delivery method: how the course will be presented

- Classroom courses.
- Webinars.
- Live.
- Recorded.
- Self-paced courses.

Schedule: when the course will be presented

- One-time date(s).
- Recurring dates.
- Available on demand.

Duration: how long the course will last

- Classroom and webinar: actual time.
- Self-paced: expected time.

Audience: to whom is the course directed

- KM team: for KM leads, project leads, and knowledge assistants.
- Users: for users who are not members of the KM team.

- Managers: targeted at managers.

Developer: who will create the course content

- In-house training: the learning and development function of your organisation.
- In-house KM team: KM lead, project lead, or knowledge assistant.
- Training firm: external company which specialises in course development.
- Consultant: KM expert (see Appendix).
- Commercially available: off-the-shelf courses available for purchase (see Appendix).

Instructor: who will deliver the course

- In-house training: the learning and development function of your organisation.
- In-house KM team: KM lead, project lead, or knowledge assistant.
- Training firm: external company which specialises in course delivery.
- Consultant: KM expert (see Appendix).
- Commercially available: off-the-shelf courses available for purchase (see Appendix).

Compliance: who needs to take the course, and how is successful completion determined

- Voluntary: no requirement to attend.
- Mandatory: participation is required and checked, but no test results are collected.
- Mastery: successful completion is tested for, and the course must be repeated until the participant passes.

Context: linkage of the course to other events

- Standalone: not part of any other event.
- New hire: part of standard on-boarding indoctrination.

- Specialty events: part of other training or conferences.
- Kickoff meetings: part of initial or annual full-organisation events.
- Staff meetings: part of regular meetings.

Publicity and enrollment: how the course will be promoted and how students can enroll in it

- Course catalogues: document which list available training.
- Websites: websites which list available training and link to enrollment system.
- Internal blogs, newsletters, and podcasts: communications vehicles for promoting the availability, schedule, and websites for training.
- E-mail messages: targeted messages announcing training, providing the details of what is expected and required, and reminding about schedules.
- Training logistics system: tool used to enroll students, record classes taken, and report on compliance.

Here are examples of plans for three courses.

Example 1: KM programme overview

Content: introduction – a high-level overview of the KM initiative and its components.
Delivery method: webinar (live, and recorded for playback).
Schedule: recurring dates – third Tuesday of every month.
Duration: 90 minutes.
Audience: users and managers.
Developer: in-house KM team.
Instructor: in-house KM team.
Compliance: mandatory – must be completed by all employees within one year.
Context: standalone.
Publicity and enrollment:

- Websites: promoted on KM home page and KM training page.
- Newsletters: listed in the events section of the weekly newsletter sent to all employees.
- E-mail messages: reminders sent to managers each month.
- Training logistics system: used for enrollment and compliance reporting.

Example 2: Knowledge capture process

Content: in-depth topic – understanding the knowledge capture policy and how to use the knowledge capture process.
Delivery method: classroom course.
Schedule: held once in each region.
Duration: one day.
Audience: users.
Developer: in-house training.
Instructor: in-house KM team.
Compliance: mastery – students must pass a test at the end in order to receive credit.
Context: part of standard new hire training.
Publicity and enrollment:

- Course catalogue: listed as part of new hire training.
- Website: described on the new hire training page.
- E-mail messages: sent to new hires.
- Training logistics system: used for enrollment.

Example 3: How to create a team space

Content: in-depth topic – how to create a team space to use for collaboration.
Delivery method: self-paced course.
Schedule: available on demand.
Duration: expected time – 30 minutes.
Audience: users.
Developer: in-house training.
Instructor: in-house training.

Compliance: voluntary.

Context: standalone.

Publicity and enrollment:

- Websites: linked to from the KM training page and from the team space creation page.
- Blogs and podcasts: mention the availability of the course and provide the link to access it.
- Training logistics system: used to record completion for use in employee development plans.

As you complete the training plan, review the Top 50 KM Components list and plan courses for all key elements of your KM programme. You can combine components into courses wherever possible.

Take advantage of commercially-available self-paced courses as much as possible – this is an example of reuse. For example, APQC (http://www.apqc.org/promos/marketing/books/BookstoreTopicList.html#KM) offers self-paced CD-ROM training on topics such as:

- Communities of practice.
- Capturing critical knowledge from a shifting work force.
- Creating a knowledge-sharing culture.
- The transfer of internal knowledge and best practice.
- Knowledge mapping.

For more information on e-learning, see 'Learning Circuits Links' by Ryann Ellis at http://www.learningcircuits.org/links.

Documentation

User guides, manuals, and help files which allow users to read about what is expected of them; the people, processes, and tools which are available to them; and how to use all of these in order to learn, share, reuse, collaborate, and innovate.

Complete and effective documentation supports training, communications, and user assistance. It is a good way to demonstrate knowledge sharing and reuse, and allows users to learn about all elements of the KM programme. The types of documentation to provide include big picture documents, user's guides, administrator's guides, policies and procedures, and knowledge sharing documents.

Big picture documents: These are conceptual or overview documents. They help users understand the importance of KM and their role in making it succeed. Intended for those interested in a high-level view of KM, why things work the way they do, and what resources are available.

Examples:

- Strategy and vision: defines the Top Three Objectives, the KM strategy, and a vision for how things should work.
- Programme governance: describes how the KM programme is governed.
- Roles: defines the roles of KM leaders, project leaders, and knowledge assistants.
- Priorities: defines the KM team's priorities for the year.
- Expectations: states the importance of KM to the organisation and specifies the responsibilities of all professionals and managers.
- Getting started: explains basic KM concepts, what resources are available, and how to learn more.
- Initiatives inventory: lists all KM initiatives in the organisation with sponsoring organisations, responsible individuals, and links to websites.
- Overview: provides highlights of the KM programme, details on all components,

and screen shots of and links to all relevant websites.

- Architecture: explains the structure of the KM environment, the standard taxonomy, how content is contributed, and how it is searched for.
- Insights: provides an overview of the topic of KM, including definitions, models, process maps, checklists, and industry examples.

User's guides: These are written to help users understand how to do something. Knowledge assistants can refer users to these when providing support.
Examples:

- FAQ (frequently asked questions): answers to the most typical questions concerning finding content, sharing, asking questions, tools, external access, communities, collaboration, archiving, expectations, time reporting, contacts, documentation, rewards, training, and support.
- How to collaborate: describes the processes and technologies that are used to encourage employees to collaborate and participate in communities.
- Communities: explains how to create, build, sustain, and participate in communities.
- Face-to-face knowledge sharing: describes why this is important, different types, guidelines, examples, suggestions, and pitfalls to avoid.
- People guides: explains how to use a particular KM people component, e.g., knowledge help desk, measurements, or incentives.
- Process guides: explains how to use a particular KM process, e.g., capture, reuse, or lessons learnt.

- Tool guides: explains how to use a particular KM tool, e.g., team space, repository, or threaded discussion.
- How to ask for help: describes the key elements of a successful request for help for those posting a question to a threaded discussion or sending an e-mail message seeking help to a large distribution list.
- How to record time: explains how time spent on KM activities should be reported in the organisation's labour tracking system.
- How to track accomplishments: describes how to track KM accomplishments in order to take credit for them during performance reviews.

Administrator's guides: These are written to help administrators and knowledge managers understand how to do something.
Examples:

- Managing disk usage in team spaces: helps team space administrators be efficient in the use of disk storage.
- Portal administrator's guide: addresses the most common issues faced by portal administrators.
- Threaded discussion moderator's guide: describes the role and duties of moderators.
- Threaded discussion administrator's guide: details every aspect of the software used for threaded discussions.
- Metadata guide: defines the standard metadata used for documents stored in repositories.

Policies and procedures: Details on standard processes which are required of users. These may be part of an official document repository, in which case, they are linked to from the KM documentation web page.

Examples:

- Collaboration policy: defines the policy for how teams are to collaborate.
- Knowledge capture and reuse policy: defines the policy for how knowledge is to be captured and reused.
- Knowledge capture and reuse procedure: details the steps to follow in support of the policy.
- Records management policy: defines the policy for how the organisation's business records are to be managed.
- Archiving procedure: details the steps to follow in support of the records management policy's archiving rules.

Knowledge sharing documents: These are written to capture tacit knowledge and convert it into explicit knowledge.
Examples:

- White Papers: brief publications about trends, insights, and knowledge nuggets.
- Methodologies and techniques: brief publications sharing tips, tricks, and how-to advice.
- Case studies: in-depth reviews of actual practices.
- Seminars and conferences: materials received at or presented at industry events, training courses, or symposia.
- Customer-ready materials: presentations designed for external audiences.

For an example of an administrator's guide, see 'UBB.Threads Software Administrator's Guide' at http://www.ubbcentral.com/support/docs/ubbthreads/UBBTadmin.html. For more information on documentation, see 'Writing for the Web' by Jakob Nielsen at http://www.useit.com/papers/webwriting/.

Communications

Vehicles for informing current and potential users about progress in the KM initiative through websites, team spaces, portals, wikis, forums, conference calls, blogs, newsletters, distribution lists, and links.

Timely communications are critical to successfully introducing a new KM initiative and to keeping the organisation informed on implementation progress. Some information needs to be communicated repeatedly, since you won't reach everyone at any one time, and some people won't pay attention even if you do reach them. So create a communications plan with both new and recycled elements to introduce new developments and remind about existing ones.

In the plan, specify the vehicles you will use to inform your organisation about the programme, including plans, roll-out, and ongoing implementation. Focus on the deliverables of the KM strategy, not the strategy itself. Provide details on your planned use of the following vehicles.

Websites: Intranet pages dedicated to the KM programme. Use as the starting point for accessing all knowledge resources.

Team spaces: Collaboration sites dedicated to the core team, knowledge assistant team, group teams, and the KM community. Use to share files, hold meetings, conduct polls, and maintain lists.

Portals: Repositories of KM documents. Use to store big picture documents, user's guides, administrator's guides, and policies and procedures.

Wikis: Intranet pages which can be edited by any user. Use for interactive editing of content by multiple people.

Threaded discussions: Bulletin board for the KM community. Use to disseminate information, ask and answer questions, and share insights.

Conference calls: Regular telephone calls for the KM community. Use for two-way communications, status updates, and learning.

Blogs: Web logs used by members of the KM core team. Use to post regular updates, solicit comments, and take advantage of syndication capability.

Newsletters: Periodicals sent to subscribers interested in KM and knowledge resources. Use to provide regular updates, success stories, and useful content to interested parties.

Podcasts: Recorded broadcasts available on demand or by subscription. Use for those who prefer audio, like to listen while performing other tasks, or who are not usually connected to the network and subscribe for automatic downloads of the broadcasts through syndication.

Videos: Recorded videos available on demand. Use for those who prefer video, when there is important visual content, or for special occasions.

Distribution lists: Lists of e-mail addresses used to distribute messages about the KM programme. Use for occasional communication of high importance, and do so infrequently to reduce information overload.

Reports: Details on how the KM initiative is performing against its goals. Use for communicating programme progress to leaders and stakeholders.

Submissions: Articles about the KM programme submitted to other newsletters. Use to inform those who may currently be unaware of the existence of your programme and point them to other available communications vehicles.

Links: Links to KM websites which appear on other websites. Use to attract visitors to the program website from other high-traffic websites.

Meetings: Face-to-face gatherings of members of the KM community. Use to build trust, establish direction, and solicit inputs.

Internal presentations: Attending meetings of other groups to deliver a KM message. Use to increase awareness, influence behaviour, and request cooperation.

External presentations: Talking about the KM programme to external audiences. Use to build credibility, demonstrate thought leadership, and receive feedback.

External publications: Publishing articles in magazines, journals, blogs, and websites. Use to increase visibility and build a positive reputation.

External conferences: Attending and presenting at industry events. Use to increase recognition, network with peers, and test ideas.

Audience surveys: Soliciting inputs from the target audience, since communication isn't just about talking – it also includes asking questions and listening. Use to determine what users like, dislike, and want changed.

The communications plan should include the following elements for each vehicle.

Type: one of the vehicles.
Content: what subjects will be covered.
Purpose: what is the objective.
Audience: to whom is the vehicle directed.
Schedule: when will the vehicle be delivered.
Author: who will create or edit the content.
Sources: where will content be obtained.
Channels: how will the message be delivered (e.g., names of distribution lists).
Contacts: who will help produce and deliver it (names, phone numbers, and e-mail addresses).
Sites: where will the content be stored (URLs) – Tip: use a URL which is easy to remember, such as km.name.com, for the KM home page.

Here are examples of plans for three vehicles.

Example 1: KM home page

Type: website.
Content: links, news, RSS feeds, site of the day, and search box.
Purpose: primary user interface to all knowledge resources.
Audience: all users of knowledge resources.
Schedule: initial version one month prior to programme launch, then continuously updated.
Author: organisation KM leader.
Sources: programme staff.
Channels: organisation intranet.
Contacts: webmaster.
Sites: km.organisation.com.

Example 2: Monthly newsletter

Type: newsletter.
Content: programme progress, user success stories, technology updates.
Purpose: keep users informed about progress, improvements, and successes.
Audience: all users of knowledge resources.

Schedule: the month of programme launch, and every month thereafter.
Author: people project leader.
Sources: core team.
Channels: subscription automation system.
Contacts: subscription automation system programme manager.
Sites: posted to KM home page as a news item, and archived on a separate page.

Example 3: Weekly blog

Type: blog.
Content: top 50 KM components.
Purpose: keep those interested in KM topics informed on internal and external developments and news.
Audience: everyone who is interested in KM and its underlying components.
Schedule: weekly.
Author: technology project leader.
Sources: newsletters, blogs, RSS feeds, website searches.
Channels: blog page and RSS feed.
Contacts: internal blog support.
Sites: internal blog site.

Here are external examples of each of the top ten vehicles. You will create internal versions of these.

- Website: AOK http://www.kwork.org /index.html
- Team space: Com-Prac http://groups. yahoo.com/group/com-prac/
- Portal: KnowledgeBoard http://www. knowledgeboard.com/index.html
- Wiki: KmWiki http://kmwiki.wikispaces.com/
- Threaded discussion: actKM http://actkm.org/mailman/listinfo/ actkm_actkm.org
- Conference call: SI KM Leaders http:// groups.yahoo.com/group/sikmleaders/

- Blog: KM Chicago http://kmchicago. blogspot.com/
- Newsletter: Gurteen Knowledge Letter http://www.gurteen.com/gurteen/ gurteen.nsf/(Views)/WebNewsList?Open Document&Count=999
- Podcasts: Dr. A.K. Pradeep on Enterprise Blogging http://www.podcastingnews. com/details/www.searchscience.com/rss. xml/view.htm
- Videos: Gurteen Knowledge @ 50 Lessons http://gurteen.50lessons.com/
- Gurteen Knowledge Conversations http://www.i-t-l.com/gurteen%5Fkcon/ index_files/slide0001.htm

Push communications
Take extra care in using push communications such as newsletters. You don't want to annoy users by sending them periodicals which they don't want. Here are guidelines to follow. Allow opting in and out. Use services which allow people to subscribe and unsubscribe easily. Send a one-time invitation to subscribe to a wide audience, and then respect the decisions of the recipients. Provide multiple alternatives, including e-mail, RSS feed, and reading online only.

Don't subscribe anyone who didn't request it. This is a serious violation of the opt-in principle. Don't send messages to people unless they want to receive them from you. Otherwise, you will be viewed as a spammer and your messages will annoy the recipients rather than please them. Make it obvious in each message you send out how to subscribe or unsubscribe. Make sure the links really work. Store an archived copy of each newsletter. In each issue, include a link to the archives. This will allow others to link to your newsletter.

Don't blanket all threaded discussions you belong to with the same message. If

a message is relevant to more than one threaded discussion, craft a brief, customised version which is specific to each forum, explain why it is relevant, and include a link to the full message which is posted elsewhere. Keep your newsletters as short as possible. For example, keep them to one page to encourage people to read them. If your newsletter contains multiple topic categories, try to include only one story per category.

Avoid sending messages with attachments. Instead, post any necessary files to an easily-accessible site and include links. Include your name in each communication so people will know who sent it and whom to contact with feedback and suggestions. This will also help build a positive reputation for you, especially if you follow the other nine guidelines.

Success stories
One type of content that should be a priority for many of your communication vehicles is the success story. These should be requested regularly from users in one of three ways. Ask all KM leaders to submit them each month and include them in the monthly newsletter. If you have a KM incentive system, request success story content as part of giving out points for desired behaviours. Monitor the community threaded discussions for testimonials of how the community helped a member in a time of need.

When capturing success stories, ask the following questions:

1. What challenges did you face?
2. What knowledge resources did you use?
3. How did you use these resources to address these challenges?
4. What was the outcome?
5. What benefits did you realise from using the resources (time saved, costs avoided,

incremental revenue, problems avoided, increased customer satisfaction, accelerated delivery, innovation, process improvement, etc.)?

6. What benefits did you and your organisation derive?
7. Did anyone else benefit as well (e.g., a community)?
8. What alternatives (instead of using the knowledge resources) did you consider?
9. Which alternatives did you try?
10. If you did not use the knowledge resources, how do you think the outcome would have been different?

Leadership communications
A critical communications requirement is to encourage the senior executive to communicate regularly about the importance of the KM programme. Here are steps you can take to ensure that this occurs.

Write memos for the senior executive to send out establishing KM goals for all employees. Write programme update memos for the senior executive to send out periodically. Ensure that the three KM goals are mentioned in all senior management messages, including mass memos, all-employee conference calls, and newsletters. Add a KM corner to the organisation's intranet home page. Ensure that KM is on the agenda of multiple senior leadership team meetings.

Ask to be included in senior management meetings to present progress and participate in the discussion. Ask to be included in senior management conference calls to present progress and participate in the discussion. Invite the senior executive to address a KM community call to discuss their KM priorities and to learn from the members. Ask the senior executive to serve as the host of the annual face-to-face meeting of the KM community and to attend some of the meeting. Ask senior managers

to act as co-hosts of mandatory webinars to train all managers in using tools, setting goals, and delivering messages.

For more information on communications, see the following free newsletters:

- Ragan's Grapevine http://www. enewsstand.net/ME2/Sites/Default.asp
- The Source for Communicators http:// www.sourcecomms.com/
- Communiqué from Chrysalis International Inc. http://www. chrysalisinternational.com/ezine.asp

User assistance and knowledge help desk

People who provide support by phone or e-mail to users, including tool consulting, finding reusable content, connecting to knowledge sources, process support, training, communication, and other assistance.

It is a worthwhile goal to create a KM environment that is simple, easy to use, and yields useful content with a minimum of effort. But inevitably, some users will perceive that tools are difficult to master, there are too many resources from which to choose, searching produces too few or too many results, or that it is difficult to connect to when not in the office. You should provide an easy way for users to contact experts on the KM environment to obtain consulting, help with finding information, and other assistance.

To ensure that users have a readily-accessible source of support, a knowledge help desk should be established. The knowledge assistants who staff this help desk can help find information, contact experts, provide training, and answer questions on people, process, and technology components.

Knowledge assistants are people who help employees use the KM environment by offering a variety of services. They can advise on how to use collaborative team spaces or how to use other KM tools. They can assist in locating reusable collateral or searching for information needed when a user is facing a deadline or not connected to the network and needs to find something out. They can find needed content and send it by e-mail.

They can help connect to other knowledge sources, either through communities or finding the right people inside or outside the organisation. They can help with knowledge capture and reuse, assisting in submitting content to repositories, and evaluating that submitted content is of acceptable quality.

They participate in ongoing training and communications; host webinars; help people with training; communicate information on a regular basis to employees. The knowledge assistant is someone to call or e-mail with a question about how to do something, where to find something, or for assistance with any process or tool.

To aid users in contacting the knowledge assistants, it's a good idea to provide a website with names, phone numbers, and e-mail addresses. You can also send out to everyone in the organisation a sticker on which users can write in the phone number of their closest knowledge assistant and stick it on their laptop or on their phone. In this way the contact information will be readily available when they need to contact the knowledge help desk.

For users who haven't engaged with the KM environment before but are wondering how to get started, one way is for them to call a knowledge assistant, mention some of the challenges they face, and let them offer advice on people, processes, and tools which address those challenges.

Some users need extra help in finding reusable content. When they are looking for materials to reuse, they can contact a knowledge assistant who is expert in

searching the knowledge repositories. This takes advantage of specialised expertise in searching, reduces time spent searching unproductively, and frees up time for other tasks.

Appoint an organisation knowledge assistant leader to coordinate efforts between all other knowledge assistants. This can be a role assigned to one of the KM leaders in addition to their other duties. Assign additional knowledge assistants for each key group within the organisation. Groups include regions, large countries, business units, functions, and major work teams. All assigned knowledge assistants should work as a team. They should provide back-up to each other, provide follow-the-sun coverage for 24/7 support, and assist each other in responding to difficult requests.

To the greatest extent possible, knowledge assistants should also actively engage with users, not just wait for calls and e-mail messages to be received. By contacting project teams, managers, and key users in the organisation to offer assistance, they can help bring the full power of all knowledge resources to bear.

For more information on help desks, see 'Setting Up Your Help Desk' by Bob Spencer at http://www.tsif.com/Articles/setting_up_your_help_desk.htm.

For more information on knowledge assistants, see 'Knowledge Advisors at Hewlett-Packard: Connecting People with Information' by Chris Riemer and Pam Coulter Enright at http://www.knowledgestreet.com/About_Us/Join_the_Conversation/K_Street_Reports/Knowledge_Street_Report_-_Knowledge_Advisors_at_HP.pdf.

Goals and measurements

Employee goals included in performance plans, and measurements to track performance against those goals and other operational indicators.

Each member of the organisation should have three simple knowledge-related goals that are easy to remember, straightforward to measure, and consistent with the Top Three Objectives. You should define personal goals, organisational targets, how employees will be measured, and how progress will be reported. Once you have defined three basic goals for employees, stick to them for at least a year. Have the senior executive communicate the goals to everyone in the organisation. Report progress against the goals in all communication vehicles. Recognise and reward those who exemplify excellence in each goal. Here are three sets of examples of knowledge goals tailored to individuals.

Software company

- Contribute a reusable code module to the repository.
- Publish a white paper.
- Lead a community of practice.

Research and development firm

- Reuse a proven practice.
- Serve as an expert in the ask the expert programme.
- Submit a lesson learnt.

Consulting firm

- Join a community of practice.
- Reuse a proposal for a customer.
- Collaborate using a team space.

Measure the goals overall for the organisation. Contribute a reusable code module to the repository: number of modules submitted; number of unique contributors divided by number of employees. Publish a white paper; number of white papers published; number of unique contributors divided by number of employees. Lead a community of practice: number of community leaders; number of unique community leaders divided by number of senior-level employees. Reuse a proven practice: number of proven practice documents downloaded; reported value of reused proven practices as reported in user surveys. Serve as an expert in the ask the expert programme: number of participating experts; number of unique experts divided by number of senior-level employees.

Submit a lesson learnt: number of lessons learnt submitted; number of unique contributors divided by number of employees. Join a community of practice: number of unique community members; number of unique community members divided by number of employees. Reuse a proposal for a customer: number of proposals downloaded; number of new proposals with reused content divided by number of new proposals. Collaborate using a team space; number of team spaces created; number of unique team space users divided by number of employees. When communicating the individual goals, spell out what each goal means in detail. Here is an example for a systems integration firm.

"We've set individual goals for all of the employees in the company. Everyone should have these goals in their annual performance plans. The first goal is capture, which means capturing the content and experience from the bids and projects which we work on. This includes such things as project summaries, lessons learnt, proven practices, white papers, bid documents, and project deliverables.

Goal number two is reuse, which means reusing content and experience from bids and projects, including sales collateral, service guides, project documents, software source code. And the third goal is participation, which means being an active member of at least one community and participating in that community's threaded discussion. This means asking questions, answering questions, and otherwise sharing your insights with members of that community."

At the end of the performance review cycle, it's useful to provide a tool for employees to use to gather data to use in their review discussions. It can prompt them to summarise their capture, reuse, and community activities. It can also link to online sources of data to back up their claims.

The following questions can be used as prompts for reviews.

- Did you have KM goals for this past year? If yes, what where they?
- How many hours did you charge as KM time during the year, and what were the most important items you produced during those hours?
- Which communities did you participate in? For each community, were you a leader/co-leader, a frequent contributor, an occasional contributor, or a reader/listener?
- Which threaded discussions did you subscribe to? How many postings and replies did you contribute during the fiscal year?
- What content did you submit to repositories?
- What content did you reuse from repositories?
- Did you have other significant KM achievements during the year?
- How did your KM activity benefit you, the organisation, and your clients?

- Are there colleagues whose knowledge sharing helped you and as a result you would like to acknowledge their help for their performance reviews?
- Are there colleagues who will acknowledge the help you provided to them through knowledge sharing?

For more information on measurements, see:

- 'Prove it: measuring the value of knowledge management' by the UK National electronic Library for Health at http://www.nelh.nhs.uk/knowledge_ management/km2/measurement.asp.
- 'European Guide to good Practice in Knowledge Management – Part 4: Guidelines for Measuring KM' at ftp://cenftp1.cenorm.be/PUBLIC/ CWAs/e-Europe/KM/CWA14924-04- 2004-Mar.pdf.

Incentives and rewards

Programmes designed to encourage compliance with goals, improve performance against metrics, and increase participation in KM initiatives – includes tangible rewards, recognition, and competitive rankings.

There are several differing schools of thought on whether or not to provide special rewards for desired knowledge behaviours. One school holds that incentives can yield short-term results when introducing a change initiative, but that the effects wear off over time. Another is that people will manipulate such programmes to gain the rewards without achieving the desired results (e.g., submit lots of documents with low quality or no reuse benefit). A third is that you need to provide incentives for people otherwise they won't do what you want. It's worth testing these assumptions with pilots for different types of programmes. Here is a review of some types of incentives you can try.

Performance ratings and salary increases
In conjunction with goals and measurements, you can specify that those who excel in achieving their KM goals will receive higher performance ratings and associated salary increases. Another option is to require that individual KM goals must be achieved in order to receive an above-average rating or increase.

For example, if a firm has three levels of performance ratings – fails to meet expectations, meets expectations, and exceeds expectations – you can specify that only those who achieve their KM goals can receive the highest rating, despite what other great accomplishments they may have. This is an effective way of obtaining everyone's attention.

Promotion requirement
For some job types, you can require that knowledge sharing behaviours be consistently demonstrated as a condition of advancement to higher-level positions. For example, technical experts, project managers, and people managers can be held accountable for providing examples of how they shared, collaborated, and innovated using components of the KM environment. If they don't provide such evidence, they are not promoted.

Communications announcing promotions should be widely distributed, and should include details on how the individuals shared their knowledge. This will provide examples for others working toward career advancement and give them something to strive for.

Tangible rewards
With the approval of your human resources function, you can give money or prizes for

the top contributors, top reusers, frequent contributors, frequent reusers, leaders, those who volunteer their time, those who achieve targets, or those selected by leaders or peers. Communicate the rules in advance so everyone will know how to win the awards. Here are ten examples of different ways to offer rewards.

- The people who submit the proven practices which are the five most reused will each win a financial reward.
- The five top project teams in terms of content reused in their projects will be allowed to attend the industry conference of their choice.
- For every five lessons learnt documents contributed which meet quality standards, an individual earns a gift certificate.
- Those who reuse content as part of three new proposals win the book of their choice.
- Those who lead a community of practice for one year win an MP3 player.
- Everyone who participates in a content creation initiative for three months or more wins a subscription to the journal of their choice.
- All members of a region which achieves its KM goals receive a bonus.
- The top ten who receive the most votes from their peers for sharing the most win a weekend trip for two.
- The top ten who receive the most votes from their leaders for outstanding knowledge-related behaviours are invited to attend a gala event.
- The top ten who receive the most points in competitive rankings (see below) win a financial reward.

The value of rewards does not have to be great in order to motivate people. The desire to compete, earn something free, and be acknowledged as a winner can be powerful incentives.

Recognition

Incentives don't have to cost anything to be effective. Just knowing that you have earned the attention, respect, and admiration of others, especially senior leaders, can be very gratifying. And you are more likely to repeat desired behaviours if you know that important people will take notice.

Among the ways to provide non-financial recognition are personal notes from leaders who notice contributions, newsletter articles about those who achieve success in using KM processes, success stories posted to websites, invitations to attend prestigious events hosted by the senior executive, scheduling time with senior technical leaders for exchanges of ideas, and being praised and asked to talk about their efforts in conference calls or meetings.

Competitive rankings

To take advantage of the competitive nature of many individuals, an incentive points system can be implemented to award points for desired behaviours, rank those earning points, and report on weekly, monthly, yearly, and lifetime standings. The points awarded can be used for recognition, tangible rewards, or for demonstrating achievement of goals for performance reviews and promotions.

Point totals can vary by task, can be claimed by filling in a form, or can be received automatically as a result of performing a task in another application. The point totals and rankings can be reported on websites, in newsletters, and via messages to employees and managers. Here's an example of how such a system can work. Create an application which

allows users to claim points for doing different types of activities, such as giving community presentations, publishing a white paper, acting as a subject matter expert for an ask the expert programme, serving as a moderator for a threaded discussion forum, and doing a variety of other knowledge-related tasks.

Each task has assigned to it a certain point value. Each time someone does one of these knowledge sharing or reuse functions, they can claim the points in the system. The points earned are displayed on a website to create a friendly competition amongst all employees. They can visit the site to see how they stack up against their peers, the idea being to create some fun, to show that people are in fact spending some of their time on KM, and to recognise them for that.

As many tasks as possible should be automated. For example, any time someone posts to a threaded discussions, they should automatically earn points for that. Every time someone subscribes to a new threaded discussion, they earn points.

Some tasks are entered manually. If you've reused content, you can go into the system, enter information about the content that was reused. You can rate the content. You can tell how it was reused, how much time you saved, and how much money you helped the company make as a result of that reuse. There are multiple benefits from such a system. Not only does it recognise people for sharing and reusing knowledge, it also provides data about the value of reuse. Since KM leaders are often asked to justify their efforts, such data can be extremely useful in responding.

Try to combine as many of these techniques as possible. For example, implement a competitive rankings system. Employees can use data from the system

during performance reviews. They can
submit details from the system when
applying for promotions. The top point
earners can be give tangible rewards. Those
who exceed a targeted point threshold
can be recognised as knowledge leaders.
Communications vehicles can provide
profiles of leaders and interviews with
details on their success stories. For more
information on incentives, see 'An update
on knowledge management incentives' by
Ted Graham at http://www.econtentinstitute.
org/issues/ISarticle.asp?id=99456&story_
id=163967171804.

Summary

You will need values which promote a
knowledge-sharing culture, knowledge
managers to lead your KM programme,
surveys to ensure you are on the right
track, social networks to connect people
with each other, communities to steward
specialty knowledge, training to ensure
users know what to do and how to do it,
documentation to explain the details, regular
communications to keep people informed, a
knowledge help desk to support users, goals
and measurements to align personal and
organisational objectives, and incentives and
rewards to recognise desired behaviours.

Chapter 8: Process components

This chapter examines the principal process components of the Top 50 KM Components outlined in Chapter 6.

- Methodologies.
- Creation.
- Capture.
- Reuse.
- Lessons learnt.
- Proven practices.
- Collaboration.
- Content management.
- Classification.
- Metrics and reporting.
- Management of change.
- Workflow.
- Valuation.
- Social network analysis.
- Appreciative inquiry.
- Storytelling.

A discussion of each component is provided, along with links for additional information.

Methodologies

Policies, rules, techniques, and procedures which prescribe how work it is to be performed and provide proven ways to do it successfully.

Once a process has been used successfully to accomplish a desired result, it can be codified to allow it to be repeated. In some cases, reusing the process is so beneficial that it becomes a prescribed policy which must be followed. Policies define what tasks must be followed in specific situations, and procedures provide the details on how these tasks are to be performed.

In other cases, useful processes are included in a collection of standard methods and templates that are provided to all those who perform similar work. Examples include methodologies for project management, software development, and research protocols. Rules define specific actions that are required, allowed, and not allowed in the context of implementing a process. Rules of thumb are insights about how to accomplish a task based on practical experience.

Techniques are methods which have been found to work to elicit information, perform analysis, solve problems, and take action in a particular area of practice. For example, the field of KM has many techniques which can be used by practitioners, many of which can be found in 'KM toolbox: inventory of tools and techniques' by the UK National electronic Library for Health at http://www.nelh.nhs. uk/knowledge_management/km2/toolkit. asp. Following are examples from the KM toolbox and other sites.

After Action Reviews were developed in the US Army and are now widely used to capture lessons learnt both during and after an activity or project. An After Action Review (http://www.skagit.com/~donclark/ leader/leadaar.html) "is an assessment conducted after a project or major activity that allows employees and leaders to discover (learn) what happened and why. It may be thought of as a professional discussion of an event that enables employees to understand why things happened during the progression of the process and to learn from that experience."

Delphi Method (http://is.njit.edu/pubs/ delphibook/) "is a group decision process about the likelihood that certain events will occur. It is a method for structuring a group communication process so that the process is effective in allowing a group of individuals, as a whole, to deal with a complex problem."

Exit Interviews (http://www.skyrme. com/UPDATES/u55_f1.htm) can be used to capture the knowledge of departing employees. Many firms conduct exit interviews, but these are usually focused purely on personnel factors. Exit interviews can be part of a KM strategy and have knowledge capture as their focus.

Knowledge Audit (http://poojasongar. com/blog/?p=6) is a systematic process to identify knowledge needs, resources, and flows as a basis for understanding where and how better KM can add value. It "helps the audited unit determine what it knows, who knows what, what it does not know, what it needs to know, and how it should improve the management of its current knowledge".

Knowledge Harvesting (http://www. knowledgeharvesting.com/) can be used to capture the knowledge of experts and make it available to others. "Knowledge harvesting converts expertise into knowledge assets. The organisation can be protected from expensive personnel losses and defections, and from the unavailability of expertise when and where needed."

Knowledge Mapping (http://www. smithweaversmith.com/knowledg2.htm) is a process "to help discover the location, ownership, value and use of knowledge; to learn the roles and expertise of people; to identify constraints to the flow of knowledge; and to highlight opportunities to leverage existing knowledge".

Mind Maps (http://www.peterussell.com/ mindmaps/mindmap.html) "were developed by Tony Buzan as a way of helping students make notes that used only key words and images. They are much quicker to make, and because of their visual quality much easier to remember and review. The non-

linear nature of mind maps makes it easy to link and cross-reference different elements of the map."

Most Significant Change (http://www. mande.co.uk/docs/MSCGuide.htm) "involves the collection of significant change stories emanating from the field level, and the systematic selection of the most significant of these stories by panels of designated stakeholders or staff. The designated staff and stakeholders are initially involved by searching for project impact. Once changes have been captured, various people sit down together, read the stories aloud and have regular and often in-depth discussions about the value of these reported changes. When the technique is implemented successfully, whole teams of people begin to focus their attention on programme impact."

Open Source (http://en.wikipedia. org/wiki/Open_source) "describes practices in production and development that promote access to the end product's source materials, typically source code. Some consider it as a philosophy, and others consider it as a pragmatic methodology."

Peer Assists (http://www.welch-consulting. com/PeerAssist.htm) were developed at BP-Amoco to learn from the experiences of others before embarking on an activity or project. "The Peer Assist is a one to two day facilitated meeting involving two groups of professionals: a team that is trying to deal with the critical business issue, and a team of subject matter or domain experts whose knowledge and experience can be tapped. The ability of the Peer Assist to tap into new expertise makes it a valuable tool that yields immediate insights and results."

Prediction Markets (http://kmblogs. com/public/item/105430) "are markets created for the purpose of making predictions. Contracts are created whose final value is tied to a particular event or outcome. The current market prices of the contracts are interpreted as predictions of the probability of the event or outcome." In "Workers, Place Your Bets" at http://www.businessweek.com/technology/content/aug2006/tc20060803_012437.htm Rachael King wrote "More corporations are setting up their own markets for economic forecasts, hoping to tap into the wisdom of employees".

World Café Conversations (http://www.theworldcafe.com/worldcafe.html) "are an intentional way to create a living network of conversation around questions that matter. A Café Conversation is a creative process for leading collaborative dialogue, sharing knowledge and creating possibilities for action in groups of all sizes."

An extensive repository of methodologies, collected both from internal and external sources, can provide users with process tools to help them do their jobs more effectively. And using the KM techniques listed above allows knowledge managers to offer practical ways of assisting others in the organisation to take advantage of their knowledge. Also see:

- 'Facilitation Resources' by Chris Corrigan at http://www.chriscorrigan.com/wiki/pmwiki.php?n=Main.FacilitationResources
- 'Common Knowledge' Associates Resources at http://commonknowledge.org/page.asp?id=30

Creation

Inventing new concepts, approaches, methods, techniques, products, services, and ideas which can be used for the benefit of people and organisations.

Many organisations would like to be known for their innovations, but it is not always easy to turn this aspiration into reality. Connecting creative people through communities, discovering patterns through analysis, and establishing processes for creating new knowledge can help stimulate innovation.

An example of knowledge creation is a patent disclosure process. When an idea for a new invention is shared with others within an organisation, it can lead to helpful suggestions for improvements, colleagues who can act as a sounding board for testing assumptions, and referrals to others doing similar work.

Another example is a process for turning practical experience into new standard methods. Provide a process for practitioners who discover improved ways of doing things to convert their insights into new methodologies, which will result in new knowledge being provided to others.

Even something as simple as regularly inviting innovators to present their latest ideas and inventions during community events can become a process of creation. As part of such presentations, build in time for the community members to brainstorm about ways to apply the concepts. Suggest that good ideas be pursued, and follow up on them during future events.

Along similar lines, providing an easy process for white papers to be submitted, reviewed, and published can facilitate knowledge creation. Provide a way to subscribe to new publications in areas of interest, connect with the authors, and collaborate on further enhancements of published ideas. Also see:

- 'Building Ba to Enhance Knowledge Creation and Innovation at Large Firms' by Ikujiro Nonaka at http://www.dialogonleadership.org/Nonaka_et_al.html

- *Enabling Knowledge Creation: How to Unlock the Mystery of Tacit Knowledge and Release the Power of Innovation* by Georg von Krogh, Kazuo Ichijo, and Ikujiro Nonaka http://www.amazon.com/gp/product/0195126165/
- *The Knowing Organization: How Organizations Use Information To Construct Meaning, Create Knowledge, and Make Decisions* by Chun Wei Choo http://www.amazon.com/gp/product/0195110129/
- *The Wealth of Knowledge: Intellectual Capital and the Twenty-first Century Organization* (http://www.amazon.com/gp/product/0385500726/) by Thomas Stewart, Chapter 9 "A New Design: Supporting Knowledge Processes 1: Processes that Create"

Capture

Collecting documents, presentations, spreadsheets, records, processes, software source, images, audio, video, and other files which can be used for learning, reuse, and innovation.

Dave Snowden asserts "If you ask them to give you your knowledge on the basis that you may need it in the future, then you will never receive it" (http://www.cognitive-edge.com/2006/08/volunteer_not_conscript.php). This suggests that it is difficult to capture knowledge. And even if you do capture it, there is no guarantee that it will be reused.

Taking these caveats into consideration, it is nonetheless useful to establish processes for capturing knowledge for later reuse. As long as you don't get carried away with attempting to capture all documents, a capture process can be helpful in providing a supply of reusable content. An example of a capture process is storing information on every project undertaken by an organisation in a project repository. This allows members of the organisation to search the database to find out if there is knowledge from previous projects which can be applied to new ones.

This can be used in multiple ways. Sometimes you need to answer the question 'have you ever done this before' when proposing a new project to a customer. Or you want to review lessons learnt from prior work. Reusing documents such as proposals, statements of work, project plans, and designs is another benefit of knowledge capture. Also, it can be helpful to contact the members of project teams to discuss their experiences, insights, and suggestions before embarking on similar efforts.

A project repository can have a fairly simple entry form for information about the project. It might include the project name, a unique identifier, customer, industry, country, solution, a brief description of the project, and a list of the team members. This may be all the information that is required, with the option to associate other documents that are project related.

Another example is a white paper capture process for tips, rules of thumb, insights, or nuggets of knowledge. These can be categorised by the type of subject, and people can subscribe to and read the white papers based on their interests. If someone has solved a particular problem or has come up with a concept which they think other people might benefit from knowing, a capture process for easily publishing their knowledge can lead to sharing and reuse.

Without such a process, it's possible that those who are known for their good ideas may be repeatedly contacted by others seeking the benefit of their experience and expertise. After the fifth or sixth time of explaining the same information over and over again, those being contacted will appreciate a way for them to capture that information so that it is in one place that everybody can access.

Also see 'Right Questions to Capture Knowledge' by Theresia Olsson Neve at http://www.ejkm.com/volume-1/volume1-issue1/issue1-art6-neve.pdf.

Reuse

Putting to practical use the captured knowledge, community suggestions, and collaborative assistance provided through knowledge sharing.

Reuse is the other side of capture. It represents the demand for the knowledge supply which results from a knowledge capture process. In order for reuse to succeed, there must be a good supply of reusable content, it must be easy to find, and it must be in a format suitable for reuse.

Knowledge capture and reuse processes are often combined into a single process which provides for both the supply and the demand for knowledge. A related policy which defines what must be captured and reused, and a related procedure which specifies how to do so should be created.

In addition to the reuse of captured documents, other reuse processes can take advantage of advice offered by communities and knowledge help desks. Many of the other KM components lend themselves to reuse, including people (training, documentation, user assistance), process (methodologies, lessons learnt, proven practices, valuation, storytelling), and technology (repository content, threaded discussion content, search results, e-learning content).

Also see 'Knowledge Reuse For Innovation – The Missing Focus In Knowledge Management: Results Of A Case Analysis At The Jet Propulsion Laboratory' by Ann Majchrzak at http://km.nasa.gov/pdf/55254main Majchrzak-Neece-Cooper-AOM-32319.pdf.

Lessons learnt

Explaining what an individual or team has learnt as a result of their experience, using documents, presentations, discussions, and recordings – including what they tried, what worked, what didn't work, what to do, what to avoid, problems faced, how problems were solved, what they would do differently, and key insights and nuggets.

It's easier to get people to talk about successes than about failures, but there is often more to be learnt from the latter. Designing a process to capture and reuse lessons learnt from both can yield great benefits.

Lessons learnt can be written down and stored in a repository, presented during a community meeting and recorded for later playback, and discussed in a roundtable on a conference call. A facilitator can collect individual lessons learnt from multiple people and compile them in a summary document.

Avoid capturing generic platitudes such as 'it's important to have a good plan' or 'involve support groups early'. Instead, look for nuggets such as 'use one extra ounce of grease to lubricate the subassembly during routine maintenance to prevent engine failure'. Provide ways for lessons learnt to be presented and discussed during community events. Don't just publish them in a document or in a database.

Once an initial collection of lessons learnt has been published, ensure that it is periodically reviewed and updated. This should be part of the standard process for capturing, publishing, and maintaining lessons learnt. Consider scheduling a separate recurring conference call during which a team or individual is asked to discuss their lessons learnt. Record the calls, and write down the best ideas for publication.

Also see 'Tips for Capturing Lessons Learned: 5 Questions to Answer with Your Team' by Adele Sommers at http://learnshareprosper.com/tools/capturing_lessons_learned.pdf.

Proven practices

Selecting, documenting, and replicating processes which have proven to improve business results so that others in similar environments or with similar needs can benefit from proven successes.

Usually referred to as best practices, proven practices are methods which have been demonstrated to be effective and lend themselves to replication to other groups, organisations, and contexts. The problem with the term 'best practice' is that it connotes that an ideal has been achieved, where 'proven practice' more reasonably asserts that an approach as been tried successfully.

At Ford, where best practice replication has been a foundation of their KM initiative within manufacturing, senior management made it a priority for plants to share their proven practices with each other so that all plants could benefit from efficiencies being realised at any one plant. When visiting one plant, the senior vice president would ask which practices had been *shared with* other plants, and which ones had been *implemented from* other plants. Each plant visit included similar questioning, and this established the importance of the process.

Communities of practice are a natural vehicle for proven practices to be shared. Threaded discussions, repositories, and community knowledge sharing events can be used to publicise proven practices and encourage their application. Document templates for proven practices should be provided so that all necessary content is captured, including process descriptions, photos, and specifications. Video recordings can be helpful in showing how a process is actually performed, and can be delivered through standard e-learning systems.

Proven practices should be as specific as possible, have obvious benefits, and be readily reproducible. Here are three Ford examples from 'Measuring the Impact of Knowledge Management' by APQC at http://www.apqc.org/portal/apqc/ksn?paf_gear_id=contentgearhome&paf_dm=full&pageselect=detail&docid=114509:

A forklift operator whose job was to transfer stacks of truck frames from a rail car to the production area, thought that there was enough space on the railcar to accommodate five stacks rather than four. Trials were conducted and the idea was proven.

A plant investigated the benefits of replacing up to 40 individual air houses on the roof with one unit. Multiple plants now have the larger units.

A product developer created a mathematical model that associated design variables and features with known customer expectations, likes, and dislikes. This predictor model was replicated across all vehicle platforms.

Consider offering a formal process for collecting, storing, disseminating, and replicating proven practices. The resultant benefits can often be used as proof of the value of a KM initiative. Also see:

- 'Identifying and sharing best practices' by the UK National electronic Library for Health at http://www.nelh.nhs.uk/knowledge_management/km2/best_practices_toolkit.asp
- 'Best practice replication: The evolution of KM at Ford Motor Company' by Stan Kwiecien at http://www.ikmagazine.com/xq/asp/articleid.D2B0DD2B-6588-442B-8C20-008AD455213E/qx/display.htm

Collaboration

Interacting with peers and colleagues to exchange ideas, share experiences, work together on projects, and solve problems.

Work teams, project teams, and communities need a consistent way to share their knowledge, coordinate their activities, and communicate with one another. Providing a process for collaboration enables basic functions such as document and photo libraries, file sharing, membership rosters, lists, discussions, polls and surveys, calendars, meeting sites, and links. Making this process a standard ensures that there is a consistent way to collaborate so that once a user has learned how to do so, it will always be the same.

A standard collaboration process ensures a predictable, reliable, backed-up, and supported environment, which is preferable to ad-hoc methods such as e-mail, shared drives, personal hard drives, or unsupported tools. The process should allow a team to continue collaborating without losing information even if one or more of the members departs, a PC is lost or stolen, or a hard drive fails.

Without a standard, collaboration will be done in a variety of sub-optimal ways, or not at all. Thus, it is desirable to define a policy which requires the collaboration process to be followed by all teams. The policy should be supported by a standard tool for collaboration with a self-service creation process which is very easy to use. Until collaboration becomes ingrained, make it one of the three goals for KM for all employees for whom it is relevant. For example, 'For every customer project, a team space using the standard collaboration tool should be created for project team collaboration'. Then report each month on progress to achieving the goal.

The combination of a quick self-service creation process for team spaces, the ease of use of the chosen collaboration tool, and an employee goal should lead to rapid and widespread adoption. As a result, you should be able to declare success and replace the collaboration goal with a different goal for the subsequent year.

A collaboration process should include a policy, procedure, standard tool, standard templates for different types of teams, training, and support. It can be supplemented with a capture process which allows reusable content to be selected from team spaces and submitted to appropriate repositories for later reuse. It's also helpful to provide guidelines for how to collaborate, including effective ways to ask others for help.

Providing a standard, supported way for teams to collaborate is a basic enabler of KM. It allows knowledge to flow between people, creates an environment where documents and ideas can be shared, and provides supporting tools such as polls which make it easy to find out what team members are thinking. Also see:

- 'Collaboration First, Then Knowledge Management' by Matthew Clapp at http://www.cmswatch.com/Feature/109
- 'Ten Rules for Asking Others to Share Knowledge' by Bruce Karney at http://km-experts.com/articles.htm

Content management

Creating, managing, distributing, publishing, and retrieving structured information – the complete lifecycle of content as it moves through an organisation.

Managing content is a key discipline which is not unique to KM, but which is definitely related. Components of a content management process include creation, presentation, information architecture, infrastructure, and governance. If your organisation produces and maintains a large quantity of documents and presentations, internal and external websites, or recordings and videos, then a content management process will be important for ensuring that content can be created, delivered, reused, maintained, and deleted effectively.

In the context of a KM programme, content management should be applied to documents, methods, and templates stored in standard repositories. It especially applies to the creation, submission, and management of reusable documents. The goals are that content is presented in a consistent format; is reviewed and approved before being made available; can be readily found through browsing, searching, and notification; and is regularly reviewed, updated, and retired. Also see:

- 'Building an Effective Content Management Strategy' by Seth Earley at http://www.earley.com/Earley_Report/ ER_CM_Strategy.htm
- Interview with Lou Rosenfeld on 'Content Management and Information Architecture' by Tony Byrne at http:// www.cmswatch.com/Feature/90
- 'Content Management Requirements Toolkit' by James Robertson at http:// www.steptwo.com.au/products/toolkit/ index.html
- 'Managing Enterprise Content' by Martin White at http://www. ark-group.com/home/xq/asp/ pubid.7988DAA9-B084-4EF8-949D- FC86FCE3C6EF/pTitle.Managing_ Enterprise_Content/qx/Publications/ Publication.htm
- Content Management Jumpstart Conference Call Series http://www. earley.com/webinars.htm

Classification

Creating and maintaining a taxonomy that can be used to organise information so that it can be readily found through navigation, search, and links between related content.

To ensure that information can be readily found, it is important to use a standard classification terminology when storing it. By defining a taxonomy before beginning to store information in repositories, and then applying the taxonomy through the use of standard metadata and tagging, future problems with inconsistent categories, conflicting and redundant metadata, and difficulty in finding content can be prevented.

Define the team which will define and maintain the taxonomy for the organisation. It should include the key content owners and the KM team members who manage the repositories.

According to Bob Bater (http://finance. groups.yahoo.com/group/TaxoCoP/ message/376), "an ontology identifies and distinguishes concepts and their relationships; it describes content and relationships. A taxonomy formalises the hierarchical relationships among concepts and specifies the term to be used to refer to each; it prescribes structure and terminology. A thesaurus provides an initial entry-point, in the user's terms, to the structured language of the taxonomy used to index documents. A classification is a taxonomy where a numerical or alphanumerical identifier has been assigned to each node to provide a means of ordering items."

Examples of taxonomies include the Dewey Decimal System for books, the organisation of living things (Kingdom, Phylum, Class, Order, Family, Genus, Species), and the Yahoo! Directory for the Web (http://dir.yahoo.com/).

A folksonomy (http://ask.metafilter. com/mefi/29264) "is the exact opposite of a taxonomy in that it is flat (that is, it has no hierarchy no parent-child relationships) and is completely uncontrolled (part of making a taxonomy is deciding what the names of your entities are, but in a folksonomy, there can be a thousand different words for the same thing). Any relationships you see in a folksonomy have to be derived mathematically (statistical clustering). However, a folksonomy is like a taxonomy in that they share the same purpose: classification." Examples of folksonomies are del.icio.us (http://del.icio.us/tag/), Technorati (http://www.technorati.com/tags/) and flickr (http://www.flickr.com/photos/tags/).

A tension exists between the common wish of users to search for information using simple text search and the need of content managers to tag and organise content so that it can located by browsing and searching. Classification of content enables it to be found, read, and understood in the appropriate context. You will need to educate users as to why classification is important to them, how to add metadata when contributing content, and how to use faceted searches (those which use metadata) to more effectively locate information.

Efforts to define an exhaustive taxonomy for an organisation can easily become so large and complex that they fail to be completed, implemented, or adopted. A bounded taxonomy for a group within an organisation will have a better chance of success. Limit the scope to the key terms which will be used as standard metadata for content classification, and then use this taxonomy for navigation menus, browsing filters, and structured search engines. Give users the option of using free text search, metadata search, navigation, browsing, or a thesaurus.

You may wish to provide users the ability to tag content themselves to create folksonomies, which can be used to complement formal taxonomies. When submitting content to repositories, make it mandatory but easy to add the required metadata, and keep this to the absolute minimum to avoid frustrating users. Also see:

- 'Taxonomy Community of Practice Wikispace' at http://taxocop.wikispaces.com/
- 'Taxonomies: Frameworks (2nd Edition)'by Jan Wyllie at http://www.ark-group.com/home/xq/asp/pubid.C052C8A4-332D-40CE-A75E-3C8C6AC8CF85/pTitle.Taxonomies_Frameworks_2nd_Edition/qx/Publications/Publication.htm
- Taxonomy and Metadata Conference Call Series http://www.earley.com/webinars.htm

Metrics and reporting

Capturing operational indicators and producing reports to communicate performance against goals, areas for improvement, and progress toward the desired state.

There is a wide spectrum of opinion about the importance of measuring KM activities. Some believe that it is essential, and want to collect data and create reports on a long list of detailed metrics. Others believe that this is a waste of time, and that effort is better spent on enabling knowledge flow.

Three different kinds of KM metrics are typically captured and reported. Goal-oriented measurements which directly relate to employee goals (see Chapter 7) allow assessment against those goals. Operational metrics are based on data captured by KM systems, and include such details as web page hits, uploads, and downloads; threaded discussion subscribers, posts, and replies; repository submissions, searches, and retrievals; and document ratings, wiki entries, and blog posts. Business impact metrics attempt to determine the return on investment (ROI) of KM initiatives, and include costs saved, costs avoided, incremental revenue, improved quality, increased customer satisfaction and retention, new business attracted, increased market share, revenue from innovations, and revenue from inventions.

Collecting and reporting on goal-oriented measurements ensures that the organisation is aware of how it is performing and that individuals can be held accountable for achieving their goals. Reports should be produced and distributed every month to track progress, reinforce good performance, and encourage improvements where needed. Reporting metrics by group within the organisation, for example, regions of the world or countries within a region, allows each group to compare its performance against other groups, and create a friendly competition to excel. Reporting metrics by individual may be limited by data privacy laws, and if allowed, transmitted confidentially to the manager for use in performance coaching and appraisals.

Operational metrics can be helpful in analysing how the KM infrastructure is being used, who is using it, and identifying areas for improvement. However, there is only so much which can be inferred from page hits, uploads, and downloads. These metrics don't indicate the value of any of these activities. If a user visits a web page, they may not find what they need there. If a document is uploaded, it may not be of any use to anyone. If a document is downloaded, it may not be reused. Follow these rules when deciding on which operational metrics to collect and report: keep the time and effort required to a minimum, automating as much of the collection, extraction, and production as possible. Ask your KM team about which metrics will help them the most. Focus on a few key metrics which relate to your overall objectives. Use the metrics to improve the KM environment and test for this in user surveys. Communicate the metrics regularly so that they influence behaviour.

Business impact metrics are potentially useful in justifying the expense of a KM programme, in garnering management support, and in communicating the value of spending time on KM activities. Anecdotes and success stories can be collected and converted into numerical values. Data can be captured in contribution repositories and incentive points systems about the value of learning, sharing, reusing, collaborating, and innovating. Processes can be created or modified to ask participants about the business impact of KM tasks. But there are few definitive ways to prove that a particular business indicator was solely influenced by KM. There are usually multiple reasons for a specific business result, and KM may be one of those reasons.

Some firms have conducted one-time surveys to prove the case for KM. For example, Caterpillar commissioned a one-time study (http://www.kmdynamics. com/newspowers.html) by an independent consulting firm to identify the benefits and ROI for two established communities of practice: Joints and Fasteners and Dealer Service Training. The results were:

- Qualitative ROI: Productivity (up 40%), Cost (reduced 25%), Speed (up 15%), Quality (up 4%).
- Tangible ROI: 200% for internal CoPs; 700% for external CoPs.

Based on these results, the Caterpillar KM programme was justified, and has been supported ever since. There is no need for ongoing collection and reporting of ROI, since it has been done once.

If there is a way for you to collect business impact metrics, then do so. They have more significance than operational metrics. But follow the same guidelines about limiting the effort involved to a reasonable amount.

Collecting and reporting on the measurements used in your KM programme will help you to communicate progress, motivate people to improve their performance, and reassure management of the value of the initiative. Keep the effort required to do so in the right balance with other projects, look for ways to continue to streamline the process, and review the reporting process annually to keep it relevant to the current state. Also see:

- 'Metrics for knowledge management and content management' by James Robertson at http://www.steptwo.com. au/papers/kmc_metrics/
- 'Methodologies for identifying knowledge value' by Paulo Petrucciani at http://www. knowledgeboard.com/lib/3443

Management of change
Developing a planned approach to change in an organisation to address anticipated obstacles and to ensure successful adoption.

As with metrics, there are varying schools of thought about the value of change management. Some believe that it is an essential part of any KM initiative. Others dismiss it as an obsolete concept. Most KM initiatives will involve significant changes to the existing behaviours, processes, and systems, so it is useful to create a change management plan.

The value of change management is that it forces you to consciously deal with the changes that will be required to enable KM to succeed. If you fail to do so, and proceed to implement new people, process, and technology components with inadequate preparation, conditioning of the organisation, and communication, then the new components may not be adopted as expected.

Most of the people components can be applied to the management of change. Instilling a knowledge-sharing culture with positive values is enabled through the work of knowledge managers, employee surveys, social networks, communities, training, documentation, communications, user assistance, goals, and rewards.

Changing existing processes and tools, and introducing new ones, are the key change elements to plan for. Analyse the potential impact of these changes, and plan to explain to the users how they will benefit, what their roles will be in implementing the changes, and how you will help them through the changes.

There may be resources within your organisation to assist you in developing and implementing a plan. If so, take advantage of these. If not, there are books and consultants who can help. Engage these resources to ensure that you have a viable plan and have considered the implications of your KM initiative and how the organisation will have to adapt in order to embrace it. Also see:

- 'Change Management Learning Center' at http://www.change-management. com/change-management-toolkit.htm
- '10 Principles of Change Management' by John Jones, DeAnne Aguirre, and

Matthew Calderone at http://www.
strategy-business.com/resiliencereport/
resilience/rr00006

- Change Management Community
  resources: articles, interviews, reviews,
  journals, journal collections and more
  at http://www.managementfirst.com/
  change_management/index.htm

Workflow

Embedding knowledge creation, capture,
and reuse in business processes so that
these steps happen routinely as part of
normal work.

Individuals do not get excited about
their organisation's attempts to manage
knowledge, and are skeptical about the
possibility of doing so. But when they need
to know something in order to do their jobs,
they want to be able to access the information
immediately. This can cause problems
because people want to find reusable content,
but they don't want to spend any extra time
contributing it. One way to address this
imbalance is to embed knowledge capture
into normal work processes.

The Workflow Management Coalition
defines workflow as the "automation of a
business process, in whole or part, during
which documents, information or tasks are
passed from one participant to another for
action, according to a set of procedural
rules". Workflow automation applies to
more than just KM, but it can be used as
part of a KM initiative to add knowledge
flow to routine business processes.

For example, when new customer
orders are entered in a company's business
management system, it should be possible
to extract customer information from that
system for use in a knowledge repository.
Users should not have to re-enter basic
information such as customer name,
industry, location, and order amount – these

should be passed along from the business
system to the KM tool.

A project management system can
be used to prompt project managers to
enter lessons learnt reports, project
summaries, and other reusable documents
at appropriate times. A Customer
Relationship Management (CRM) system
can be used to find details about customer
references. The employee expense reporting
system can be used to enforce the capture
of required content by not authorising
reimbursement payments until that content
has been submitted.

Clever use of workflow can enable
knowledge to be presented at opportune
times for applying it. For example, a
sales representative enters a request
for presales support into a system, and
is provided with links to websites and
documents relevant to the requested topic.
Later, once the sale has been closed, the
rep enters a request for commission
payment into another system, and is
prompted to enter data into a form which
captures lessons learnt about the deal.

As much as possible, avoid the need
for users to visit a separate KM system and
instead, allow them to use other business
systems to create, capture, and reuse
knowledge. If you can make these processes
as transparent as possible to your users, you
will simplify their tasks and increase their
satisfaction with the environment. Also see:

- 'Workflow: An Introduction' by Rob Allen
  at http://www.wfmc.org/information/
  Workflow-An_Introduction.pdf
- The Workflow Management Coalition
  (WfMC) at http://www.wfmc.org/
- 'Is workflow the wrong metaphor?'
  by James Robertson at http://www.
  steptwo.com.au/papers/cmb_
  noworkflow/index.html

- 'A Course on Workflow Management' by Eindhoven University of Technology at http://www.workflowcourse.com/

Valuation

Quantifying the value of reuse and innovation so that it can be fully appreciated by the organisation, including customer pricing, cost benefit analysis, and project justification.

Assigning a value to your organisation's intellectual assets can help realise incremental revenue from sales to customers, support investments in knowledge creation and capture, and justify investments in your KM programme.

Explicitly defining the value of the reusable component of what you are selling to a customer allows you to use this value for competitive pricing, for additional profit margin, or to be set aside to fund additional knowledge creation and capture. To identify the value of reusable intellectual capital, ask the providing source for a suggested price, estimate the time and effort it would take to create from scratch, and the research the market value of the asset. Combine this information into an overall estimated value, and use this to set the price. Whenever the price is higher than it would have been without adding the value of reuse, this incremental amount should be recorded and compiled as one source of the financial impact of the KM programme.

Many organisations require cost benefit analysis before approving new investments and development projects. This is often true of the Information Technology function, which is faced with a multitude of requests for new systems or enhancements to existing systems. If investments involve intangible assets, it is difficult to use traditional methods to determine the projected ROI. Using the techniques described in the resources listed below can help in providing the requested cost benefit analysis. Also see:

- 'Measuring knowledge capital' by Chetan Parikh at http://www.go2cio.com/articles/index.php?id=1474
- Intellectual Capital Start Page at http://www.intellectualcapital.nl/
- Intellectual Capital Reading List http://www.klminc.com/readinglist.html
- 'The value of intellectual capital' at http://www.valuebasedmanagement.net/faq_do_intangible_assets_create_value.html
- 'Intellectual capital ROI: a causal map of human capital antecedents and consequents' by Nick Bontis at http://www.business.mcmaster.ca/mktg/nbontis//ic/publications/JICBontisFitz-enz.pdf

Social network analysis

Mapping and measuring of relationships and flows between people, groups, organisations, animals, computers or other information/knowledge processing entities; the nodes in the network are the people and groups while the links show relationships or flows between the nodes – provides both a visual and a mathematical analysis of human relationships (from Valdis Krebs).

In *The Hidden Power of Social Networks: Understanding How Work Really Gets Done in Organizations* (http://www.amazon.com/gp/product/1591392705) Rob Cross and Andrew Parker describe the benefits of using social network analysis (SNA), including:

- Improving effectiveness of functions or business units. SNA can help leaders assess the extent to which collaborations throughout their unit are aligned with strategic objectives and generating measurable business value.

- Promoting lateral coordination throughout an organisation. SNA can help identify opportunities in networks that span functions, geographies, or process steps.
- Driving innovation in new product development, R&D, or market-facing functions. SNA can isolate how and where leveraging expertise in a network will either support or impede innovation efforts.
- Facilitating large-scale change or merger integration. SNA pre-change can identify key players to work through and retain. During the change, it can inform key interventions. After the change, it can ensure appropriate integration.
- Supporting Communities of Practice. SNA can help to rapidly form and improve effectiveness of communities by working through the network to more efficiently improve collaboration and business results.
- Forming strategic partnerships or assessing client connectivity. SNA can illuminate the effectiveness of external ties to strategic partners or clients in terms of information flow, knowledge transfer, and decision-making.
- Talent management and leadership development. SNA can help improve leadership effectiveness and replicate high performance throughout an organisation.

You can use SNA to bridge silos, create awareness of distributed expertise distributed in the network, and identify and draw in peripheral network members. In 'Building Smart Communities through Network Weaving' at http://www.orgnet.com/

BuildingNetworks.pdf Valdis Krebs and June Holley assert that "improved connectivity is created through an iterative process of knowing the network and knitting the network". SNA enables you to know the network so that you can then proceed to weave new members into it.

In his profile at http://www.networkweaving.com/valdis.html Valdis Krebs advises to "connect on your similarities and profit from your diversities". By using SNA to identify those with both similarities and differences, and using this information to better connect those people, you can enable greatly improved collaboration and knowledge flow within and across organisations. SNA is especially useful in understanding and improving the social networks of individuals, in enabling more effective collaboration by ensuring that the right people are included, and in starting, building, and extending communities.

Two related processes are Organisational Network Analysis (ONA) and Value Network Analysis (VNA). Patti Anklam (http://www.byeday.net/ona.htm) defines ONA as "tools that provide managers with a visual map of the connections between and among individuals, groups, and organisations. ONA also provides quantitative data that substantiate the maps and their underlying patterns. Interviews conducted before and after the data gathering analysis ensure that the data are positioned in the context of the organisation and will not be misinterpreted or misused."

Verna Allee (http://www.value-networks.com/) defines VNA as "a business modeling methodology that visualises business activities and sets of relationships from a dynamic whole systems perspective". She further states (http://www.proofofvaluenetwork.com/eog/povsite.nsf/wwwVwContent/l2valuenetworkanalysis.htm) "the Value

Network approach helps individuals and work groups better manage their interactions and address operational issues, such as balancing workflows or improving communication. It also scales up to the business level to help forge stronger value-creating linkages with strategic partners and improve stakeholder relationships." Also see:

- University of Virginia Network Roundtable at https://webapp.comm. virginia.edu/networkroundtable/
- 'Masterclass: Social-network Analysis' by Patti Anklam at http://www.byeday. net/downloads.htm
- 'The Social Network Toolkit' by Patti Anklam at http://www.ark-group.com/ home/xq/asp/pubid.069D6399-B3E4- 4022-9735-2EC0679F21CF/pTitle. SocialNetwork_toolkit/qx/Publications/ Publication.htm
- 'Introduction to Social Network Analysis' by Valdis Krebs at http://www. orgnet.com/sna.html
- 'Suggested tools for visualizing/analyzing value networks' by Oliver Schwabe at http://groups.google.com/group/ Value-Networks/browse_thread/thread/ efd7280ac6bdb8f3/cfc0606ce2f4221d ?lnk=gst&q=schwabe&rnum=6#cfc06 06ce2f4221d
- 'Theories and methods for understanding human social networks' by Garry Robins and Pip Pattison: a complete course on SNA with slides and notes at http://www. psych.unimelb.edu.au/research/labs/ UHSN_lab.html
- 'A Network Analysis of the actKM Community of Interest' by Graham Durant-Law (slides 48 and 49 list books which will help you gain a thorough understanding) at http://www. durantlaw.info/presentations_papers/

actKM%20Jan-Jun%202006%20 Network%20v2.pdf
- 'Social Network Analysis' by Peter Morville at http://www. semanticstudios.com/publications/ semantics/000006.php

Appreciative inquiry

Asking questions that strengthen a system's capacity to apprehend, anticipate, and heighten positive potential – mobilisation of inquiry through the crafting of the 'unconditional positive question'.

A cofounder of appreciative inquiry, David Cooperrider of Case Western Reserve University, states "In my view, the problem-solving paradigm, while once incredibly effective, is simply out of sync with the realities of today's virtual worlds. Problem-solving is painfully slow (always asking people to look backwards historically to yesterday's causes); it rarely results in new vision (by definition we say something is a problem because we already implicitly assume some idea, so we are not searching to create new knowledge of better ideals, we are searching how to close gaps), and, in human terms, problem-solving approaches are notorious for generating defensiveness (it is not my problem but yours)."

As a method of change, appreciative inquiry differs from traditional problem-solving approaches. The basic assumption of problem-solving is that people and organisations are fundamentally broken and need to be fixed. The process usually involves identifying key problems, analysing the root cause of failure, searching for possible solutions, and developing an action plan.

In contrast, the underlying assumption of appreciative inquiry is that people and organisations are evolving and growing.

Appreciative inquiry focuses the whole organisation on identifying its positive core – its greatest assets, capacities, capabilities, resources, and strengths – to create new possibilities for change, action, and innovation. The steps include discovering the organisation's root causes of success, envisioning bold new possibilities for the future, designing the organisation for excellence through dialogue, and co-creating the future.

In 'Creative Strategic Planning: Appreciative Inquiry' at http://www. breakthroughcreativity.com/nl_2006june. html#article1 Lynne Levesque lists five steps:

1. Definition of the focus of the work. What are we exploring or inquiring into?
2. Discovery, through the use of an interview protocol, to explore the factors that contribute to optimum performance and best individual experiences.
3. Dreaming of what could be if the exceptional moments identified in the discovery phase became normal practice.
4. Designing what specifically will be different in the future.
5. Delivering those results through a plan to move forward.

She concludes "Appreciative inquiry is not only an incredibly useful tool for strategic planning, change management, and resolving challenges. It is also applicable as a good coaching practice. Leaders who use probing questions in an appreciative mode that generates collaborative learning will see long-lasting behaviour changes."

Use Appreciative inquiry to help make the corporate culture more positive, get the best out of collaboration and communities, and to evolve from problem-solving to innovation. This process can

be applied in almost any context, and the philosophy can be applied in communities, training, communications, user assistance, rewards, lessons learnt, proven practices, collaboration, and management of change. Also see:

- Appreciative Inquiry Commons at http:// appreciativeinquiry.case.edu/
- Creative Leadership Tools at http://www. breakthroughcreativity.com/tools.html
- OvationNet: Appreciative Inquiry Online Workshops and AI Learning & Consulting Tools at http://www. ovationnet.com/

Storytelling

Using narrative to ignite action, implement new ideas, communicate who you are, build your brand, instill organisational values, foster collaboration to get things done, share knowledge, neutralise gossip and rumour, and lead people into the future (from Steve Denning).

In 'The Leader's Guide to Storytelling' at http://www.stevedenning.com/ Leader-Ch-0-TContents.pdf Steve Denning defines eight narrative patterns of organisational storytelling:

Motivate others to action: Using narrative to ignite action and implement new ideas. The challenge of igniting action and implementing new ideas is pervasive in organisations today. The main elements of the kind of story that can accomplish this – a springboard story – include the story's foundation in a sound change idea, its truth, its minimalist style, and its positive tone.

Build trust in you: Using narrative to communicate who you are. Communicating who you are and so building trust in you as an authentic person is vital for today's leader. The type of story that can accomplish this is typically a story that focuses on a turning point in your life. It has a positive tone and is told with context.

Build trust in your company: Using narrative to build your brand. Just as a story can communicate who you are, a story can communicate who your company is. A strong brand is a relationship supported by a narrative. It's a promise you have to keep, that begins by making sure that the managers and staff of the organisation know and live the brand narrative. The products and services that are being offered are often the most effective vehicle to communicate the brand narrative to external stakeholders.

Transmit your values: Using narrative to instill organisational values. The nature of values includes the differences between robber baron, hardball, instrumental and ethical values, between personal and corporate values and between espoused and operational values. Values are established by actions and can be transmitted by narratives like parables that are not necessarily true and are typically told in a minimalist fashion.

Get others working together: Using narrative to foster collaboration to get things done. The different patterns of working together include work groups, teams, communities and networks. Whereas conventional management techniques have difficulty in generating high-performing teams and communities, narrative techniques are well suited to the challenge.

Share knowledge: Using narrative to transmit knowledge and understanding. Knowledge-sharing stories tend to be about problems and have a different pattern from the traditional well-told story. They are told with context, and have something traditional stories lack, i.e., an explanation. Establishing the appropriate setting for telling the story is often a central aspect of eliciting knowledge-sharing stories.

Tame the grapevine: Using narrative to neutralise gossip and rumour. Stories form the basis of corporate culture, which comprises a form of know-how. Although conventional management techniques are generally impotent to deal with the rumour mill, narrative techniques can subvert neutralise untrue rumours by satirising them out of existence.

Create and share your vision: Using narrative to lead people into the future. Future stories are important to organisations, although they can be difficult to tell in a compelling fashion since the future is inherently uncertain. The alternatives available to a leader in crafting the future story include telling the story in an evocative fashion and using a shortcut to the future. Others include simulations, informal stories, plans, business models, strategies, scenarios and visions.

In Business Innovation Factory's 'Storytelling and the Innovation Paradox' at http://www.businessinnovationfactory.com/index.php?option=com_content&task=view&id=176&Itemid=109 Denning states "The biggest challenge in innovation is not in generating more ideas, it's about how you take the really good ideas and make them actually happen". A company's sustainability, Denning argues requires a commitment to transformation via disruptive growth – a place where most companies do not excel. The paradox, Denning finds, lies within the heart of the organisation itself. "Innovation is less about understanding the problem than getting people to act differently, often contrary to well-established assumptions and practices," he says. Denning argues that to solve this paradox, a different kind of leadership is needed – one that goes beyond the familiar command and control. By crafting a logical narrative and testing a potential new business model against it, leaders learn to adapt the innovation to the evolving realities of the marketplace.

In Business Innovation Factory's 'Thought Leaders' at http://www. businessinnovationfactory.com/index. php?option=com_content&task=view&id= 251&Itemid=113 Denning says "One of the key skills of any innovator is to communicate to the organisation the risks in clinging to the *status quo* and the potential rewards of embracing a radically different future. The nature language for accomplishing this is artful narrative – that is, telling a story about the path to a desired future in a way that fully engages the listener."

Storytelling should be incorporated in many of the KM implementation steps, activities, and components. A springboard story should be used to motivate the senior executive to approve the KM initiative and provide the Top Ten Commitments. As described in the two Business Innovation Factory articles, narrative plays an important role in innovation.

Communities can be nurtured by having members tell stories of who they are and knowledge-sharing stories about what they have learnt. The effectiveness of training and communications will be enhanced by using narratives rather than dry bullet points. For example, instead of creating the usual PowerPoint slides to present the KM programme, tell the stories of some typical users and how they apply

the components of the KM programme to help them do their jobs.

Lessons learnt can be captured and reused with greater impact if they are told as stories rather then captured as imperatives in text format. Proven practices captured as pictures, video, and audio telling the story of how to apply them will be easier to replicate than if they are in a written document. Collaboration can be stimulated by using narrative to get others working together. Almost all forms of narrative are useful in the management of change, including motivating others to action, building trust, transmitting values, getting others working together, taming the grapevine, and creating and sharing a vision.

Appreciative Inquiry is based on storytelling. In 'Five Theories of Change Embedded in Appreciative Inquiry' at http:// www.gervasebushe.ca/ai5.htm Gervase Bushe writes "The key data collection innovation of appreciative inquiry is the collection of people's stories of something at its best. If we are interested in team development, we collect stories of people's best team experiences. If we are interested in the development of an organisation we ask about their peak experience in that organisation. If enhanced leadership is our goal, we collect stories of leadership at its best. These stories are collectively discussed in order to create new, generative ideas or images that aid in developmental change of the collectivity discussing them." He continues "There is something about telling one's story of peak organisational experiences, and listening to others, that can make a group ready to be open about deeply-held desires and yearnings". Also see:

- 'Learn organisational storytelling' by Steve Denning at http://www. stevedenning.com/learn.htm

- Anecdote's Storytelling Archives at http://www.anecdote.com.au/archives/storytelling/
- Seth Kahan's interviews and papers at http://www.sethkahan.com/resources.html

Summary

The processes described in this chapter – methodologies, capture, reuse, lessons learnt, proven practices, collaboration, content management, classification, metrics and reporting, management of change, workflow, valuation, social network analysis, Appreciative Inquiry, and storytelling – all have a role in supporting KM. You will need some of these to start a KM initiative, and should consider introducing others as your programme matures. Being aware of all of these processes will allow you to incorporate elements of each into other components. This chapter provides an overview of each process, and the links provide sources for more in-depth understanding.

Chapter 9: Technology Components

This chapter examines the principal technology components of the Top 50 KM Components outlined in Chapter 6.

- User interface.
- Intranet.
- Team spaces.
- Virtual meeting rooms.
- Portals.
- Repositories.
- Bulletin boards and threaded discussions.
- Expertise locators and ask the expert.
- Metadata and tags.
- Search engines.
- Archiving.
- Blogs.
- Wikis.
- Podcasts.
- Syndication and aggregation.
- Social software.
- External access.
- Workflow applications.
- Process automation applications.
- E-learning.
- Subscription management.
- Incentive points tracking.
- Survey and metrics reporting automation.

A discussion of each component is provided, along with links for additional information.

User interface

The point of entry to a knowledge base that provides navigation, search, communication, help, news, site index, site map, and links to all tools.

To make it easy for users to access the people, process, and technology components offered by your KM programme, provide an intranet or portal site with obvious links to the available resources. Allow users to quickly navigate to the appropriate sites based on their role, business process stage, and current requirements.

The principles of good usability should be incorporated into the user interface. Here are some specific suggestions for doing so. Keep the size of the home page to a single page without the need for horizontal or vertical scrolling. The page should load quickly, be visually appealing, and be as simple as possible. Provide direct links to the most important sites so that multiple clicks through intermediate sites are unnecessary. Don't make users visit multiple sites to reach to the one they need. Remove all static information such as mission statements so that only dynamic news and useful links appear. Emphasise practical over political content. Avoid overwhelming users with long menus of links which appear on the page. Provide nested drop-down menus in a horizontal navigation bar which is replicated on each page within the site.

On each page within the site, include standard elements in the same location. These include standard banners, footers, and navigation bars. The banner should include a search box, a people look-up box, and one or two other essential links and boxes that are used so frequently that they belong in the banner. The footer should include the date last modified, the page owner, and links for feedback and support. Standard navigation elements include a horizontal navigation bar with drop-down menus and bread crumbs which show where you are in the web hierarchy and allow direct navigation to any higher level in the hierarchy.

Offer faceted navigation, browsing, and searching to guide users based on the standard taxonomy. See 'Use of

Faceted Classification' at http://www. webdesignpractices.com/navigation/facets. html for more information. Use a site map to show the overall web structure and all available pages in a single view. See 'Site Map Usability' at http://www.useit.com/ alertbox/20020106.html for design tips.

Provide an index to allow users to look up any desired topic alphabetically. Include synonyms as in a thesaurus so that regardless of which term a user chooses, they will be guided to the right place. For example, under the B section, you might include 'Bulletin Boards – see Threaded Discussions'.

Create a unique icon for each resource, and use it to brand the associated site. Keep all of these icons in a table, and every day, feature one of them on the home age with a link to the associated site. This will serve as a reminder to users about the existence of resources, draw them in through the icon, and lead them to the site.

Include links to the most visited sites, most downloaded documents, and most searched-for content. These can be updated automatically or through a monthly refresh process based on the web statistics in monthly usage reports. Provide a portion of the page to recognise people who demonstrate the desired knowledge-sharing behaviours. This can be a listing of the top ten incentive point holders, pictures of active community members, or success stories of practitioners.

Include a few news items, and provide links for subscribing to notifications, newsletters, and syndicated RSS feeds and podcasts. Keep the news fresh, and archive items regularly. Post links to the latest issues of relevant newsletters. Prominently feature links to training, documentation, help, and support. If you offer a knowledge help desk, design an attractive logo for it and feature

that link on all pages. Include the latest key metrics, and links to more detailed reports. Compare actual results to targets to celebrate progress and remind users of goals still to be achieved.

Create a Knowledge Map which includes the key resources with an icon for each, their descriptions, and links to each one. Map these resources to the different user roles, business process stages, and knowledge requirements. This should answer the question 'where do I go if I play role X, am in stage Y, and have need Z'. For example, I am a software developer, I am testing software code, and I need a standard test suite. The Knowledge Map should allow users to quickly zero in on this set of conditions and link to the required knowledge component. Also see:

- Usability.gov: your guide for developing usable and useful websites at http://www.usability.gov/
- User Interface Engineering (Jared Spool) at http://www.uie.com/
- useit.com (Jakob Nielsen) at http://www.useit.com/

Intranet

A private computer network that uses Internet protocols, network connectivity, and possibly the public telecommunication system to securely share part of an organisation's information or operations with its employees (from Wikipedia).

Your organisation's intranet is typically used to provide the user interface, including web pages, standard look and feel, navigation, and search. If you have specialised tools such as portals, team spaces, and repositories, they are usually linked to from the intranet and may be considered extensions of the intranet. In that case, you may wish to tailor these tools so that they appear to users as if they are standard intranet sites. This will minimise confusion, offer consistent navigation and search, and reduce the likelihood of the KM environment being viewed as non-standard.

The intranet is typically accessible to all employees, and also to contractors and partners who have signed appropriate nondisclosure agreements. Being a part of the intranet provides a way for users to navigate to your KM site, find its content using organisation-wide search, and take advantage of standard templates for headers, footers, and menus.

If your intranet offers a best bets feature for common searches, take the time to submit likely search terms such as 'KM', 'knowledge management', 'collaboration', and all other key components of your programme. This will help direct users to your site and reduce the need to navigate using complex hierarchies.

If your organisation does not have an intranet, or if it spans multiple entities, then the Internet provides a similar function. Tools for all of the technology components are offered to the public over the Internet, many of which are available for free or for a low cost. For any of the following tools, type 'free' before the type of tool into an Internet search engine, and multiple results should be returned. Also see:

- Books on portals at http://www.amazon. com/s/ref=nb_ss_gw/?url=search-alias%3Daps&field-keywords=intranet
- Intranet Journal at http://www. intranetjournal.com/

Team spaces
Collaborative workspaces designed to allow teams to share documents, libraries, schedules, and files; conduct meetings,

calls, surveys, and polls; and store meeting minutes, discussions, reports, and plans.

Work teams, project teams, and communities all require tools which support collaboration. A team space is a site which enables team members to post and retrieve files, share information, and carry out group activities. If teams don't have such a tool, they are faced with the need to send more e-mail to one another, difficulty in locating required documents, and the possibility of losing access to critical information when one of the team members is unavailable or leaves the organisation.

Using file shares, shared drives, and other *ad hoc* storage mechanisms is an unreliable way to collaborate. Providing a standard, readily-accessible, predictable, and backed-up environment enables effective and enduring collaboration to occur. Following are guidelines for offering, creating, and using team spaces.

Make it fast and easy to create a team space using a self-service intranet site. Provide standard templates for work teams, project teams, and communities to use when creating new team spaces. These templates can provide a consistent look and feel, useful links, and required documents. Establish and communicate rules for allowable file types, back-up frequency, and storage quotas. Regularly communicate to users about inactive team spaces, storage usage, and maintenance schedules.

Define the team members and provide access for each of them. Define at least two administrators for each team space. Provide a team roster page where members can post their photos, add links to personal sites, and describe their roles. Establish rules that all files will be shared by posting to the team space, not by sending as e-mail attachments. Remind new users about how to do this.

Set up recurring meetings in the team space so that for each meeting, there is a web page with the agenda, attendees, action items, and shared documents. Allow users to add their names to the attendee list. Allow users to subscribe to alerts to be notified when new documents are posted to the team space or when other changes are made. Use polls to conduct surveys, take votes, and made decisions.

Discourage team collaboration from taking place outside the team space. For example, project team members should not maintain any files on other sites. Create a process for deciding on which files are kept in the team space, posted to reusable document repositories, archived, and deleted. Ensure that the process is followed. For team spaces within a private intranet, see:

- EMC eRoom at http://software.emc. com/microsites/eRoom/index.jsp
- Groove Virtual Office at http://www. groove.net/home/index.cfm
- IBM QuickPlace at https://www-1.ibm. com/collaboration/quickplace/
- Livelink ECM Collaboration at http:// www.opentext.com/2/sol-products/sol-pro-docmgmt-collaboration/pro-ll-collaboration.htm
- Microsoft Windows SharePoint Services at http://www.microsoft.com/technet/ windowsserver/sharepoint/
- Vignette Collaboration at http://www. vignette.com/

Of these, SharePoint has become a very popular choice. See *Teach Yourself Microsoft SharePoint 2003 in 10 Minutes* by Colin Spence and Michael Noel at http://www. amazon.com/dp/0672327236/ to learn more about this tool.

For public team spaces available on the Internet, see:

- Google Groups at http://groups.google.com/
- MSN Groups at http://groups.msn.com/
- Yahoo! Groups at http://groups.yahoo.com/

For file sharing above the limits set by these free providers, you can use a free service such as Uploading.com (http:// www.uploading.com/). Typical usage rules require that a file be downloaded at least once every 30 to 60 days to ensure that it remains available.

Virtual meeting rooms

Online, real-time tools designed to allow teams to share presentations, applications, and white boards during meetings.

Virtual teams have become widespread. In the past, teams were often located in the same location and could meet in person whenever they wanted. Now they are often widely distributed across geographies, may never have met the other team members in person, and communicate primarily through e-mail, instant messaging, and telephone calls.

Conference calls are typically used for virtual teams to meet regularly. To enhance the sharing that can be done during a conference all, virtual meeting rooms allow participants to view common presentations, share applications, and write on virtual white boards. Microsoft NetMeeting provides some basic capabilities for small teams, but performance quickly degrades as the number of users increases above ten, and it is vulnerable to sluggish network performance.

Team spaces can be used effectively for typical presentations by posting them in the meeting space prior to the conference call, asking participants to download the files, and having presenters regularly refer to the current slide number. This avoids the need for a virtual meeting room.

When a live demonstration will be performed, when notes will be taken that need to be shared in real time, or when there is a need for video or other dynamic visual content, then a virtual meeting room or video conference is required. Web conferencing tools include:

- HP Virtual Rooms at http://education. hp.com/hpvr/
- IBM Lotus Sametime at http://www.ibm. com/lotus/sametime
- Microsoft Office Live Meeting at http:// www.microsoft.com/uc/livemeeting/
- WebEx at http://www.webex.com/

Recent advances in video conferencing technology more closely approximate face-to-face meetings. Two examples of such high-quality video conferencing tools are:

- Cisco TelePresence at http://www.cisco. com/en/US/netsol/ns669/networking_ solutions_solution_segment_home.html
- HP Halo at http://www.hp.com/halo/ index.html

Portals

Websites that provide personalised capabilities to users through the use of customisation, building blocks, and integration of multiple sources.

The term 'portal' has taken on several meanings. It can be a gateway website offering an array of services, a personalised home page which aggregates content from multiple sources, a document repository, or a sophisticated customisable user interface.

Web portals such as Excite, Yahoo!, MSN, Google, and AOL are typically free and can be personalised on the Internet.

Google continues to offer new modules which can be integrated as components on a personal home page. Enterprise portal vendors offer tools which promise to integrate diverse content through a highly-personalised user interface and advanced search capabilities. These portals are often positioned as KM tools. Here are the leading enterprise portals:

- Autonomy Portal-in-a-Box at http://www. autonomy.com/content/Products/PIB/ index.en.html
- BEA AquaLogic User Interaction at http://www.bea.com/framework. jsp?CNT=index.htm&FP=/content/ products/aqualogic/user_interaction/
- IBM WebSphere Portal at http://www. ibm.com/websphere/portal
- Microsoft SharePoint Portal Server at http://www.microsoft.com/office/ sharepoint/prodinfo/
- Open Text Livelink Enterprise Portal at http://www.opentext.com/2/sol-products/sol-pro-enterprise-portals.htm
- Oracle Portal at http://www.oracle.com/ technology/products/ias/portal/
- Vignette Portal at http://www.vignette.com/

Also see:

- Books on portals at http://www.amazon. com/s/ref=nb_ss_gw/?url=search-alias%3Daps&field-keywords=portals
- Portals Magazine at http://www. portalsmag.com/
- KMWorld Buyers Guide: Portals http:// www.kmworld.com/BuyersGuide/

Repositories

Structured lists and databases which allow documents and other files to be stored, searched for, and retrieved.

A knowledge capture process requires a place to store what is collected. A repository is such a place, designed to be easy to use for storing and retrieving content. It can take the form of a database, a list or document library within a tool such as Microsoft SharePoint, or a collection of files within an intranet site, team space, or portal.

When creating a knowledge repository, decide on what type of content needs to be captured. Plan for storage capacity which will remain adequate even as the number of collected files increases dramatically. Define the metadata which will be required for each submitted file. Decide on a structure: hierarchical folders, different list views, faceted taxonomy navigation, or metadata-based search. Specify a contribution process. Ensure that search can be properly integrated so that contributed content can be found. Consider publishing the list of the latest submissions, providing alerts for posted material, and otherwise highlighting new content so that users are made aware of it.

Examples of repositories include project databases which capture key information on all projects, customer support knowledge bases which capture problem resolutions, and proposal libraries which provide an archive of all customer proposals. In addition to providing a way for users to browse and search to find content, repositories are also useful in conjunction with threaded discussions. When a community member asks if a specific type of content is available, another member can reply with links to instances within existing repositories. This is an example of combining collection with connection; content has been collected and stored in a repository, and a connection is made between people to take advantage of that content at the time of need.

Also see books on knowledge repositories at http://www.amazon.com/s/ref=nb_ss_gw/?url=search-alias%3Daps&field-keywords=knowledge+repositories

Bulletin boards and threaded discussions

Forums for carrying on discussions among subscribers on a specific subject, including online and e-mail posts and replies, searchable archives, and discussions grouped by threads to show the complete history on each topic.

Threaded discussions provide benefits to their subscribers and to the organisation. They enable subscribers to learn from other members; share new ideas, lessons learnt, proven practices, insights, and practical suggestions; reuse solutions through asking and answering questions, applying shared insights, and retrieving posted material; collaborate through conversations and interactions; and innovate through brainstorming, building on each other's ideas, and keeping informed on emerging developments.

The organisation benefits by having a reliable place where people with questions and problems can be directed to find answers and solutions, a searchable archive of the discussions, and a way for people to learn about their specialty and to develop in it. The broader the membership in a threaded discussion, the greater the benefit to the organisation. This is due to having the widest possible range of perspectives, the greatest possible number of people to answer questions and solve problems, and greater leverage of all knowledge shared.

Providing a way for questions to be asked and answers to be supplied is a key function of threaded discussions. Subscribers post questions such as 'has anyone done this before?', 'does anyone know how to do this?', and 'where can I find this?', and other subscribers respond with answers, suggestions, and pointers to more information.

Another use of threaded discussions is sharing insights, techniques, and innovations with community members. Posting a tip on how a problem was solved, a customer was helped, or a breakthrough was achieved allows many others to reuse that knowledge in other contexts. When used in conjunction with community events, repository contributions, and published articles, threaded discussions allow communities to reflect on the events, provide feedback on the contributions, and debate ideas in the articles. This extends the useful life of events, publicises submitted content, and stimulates the lively exchange of ideas.

E-mail is the killer application for communications, and threaded discussions are the killer application for communities. There is a connection between these two applications: threaded discussion tools need to allow for reading and posting entirely by e-mail. When selecting or implementing such a tool, be sure that full e-mail functionality is provided so that subscribers will not have to visit an online site in order to participate in discussions. Allowing users to choose between e-mail or online interaction is valuable; both options should be provided.

If your organisation has people who don't all speak the same language, you may wish to implement threaded discussions in varying local languages. If English is the organisation's main language, then for topics of worldwide interest, ensure that at least one subscriber who speaks English well is assigned to subscribe to the corresponding English language discussion. Then, if something important is discussed in

the English version, the assigned translator can relay this to the local language version, and *vice versa*.

There are guidelines for threaded discussions to keep them operating effectively. Here are three typical problems in how people post to threaded discussions along with recommended solutions. Some subscribers reply to posts or digests without deleting the original text. When replying to a post, include just the text you wish to quote in response, and delete the rest. This will prevent the discussion from being cluttered with redundant text, and will make it easy to distinguish between new and old posts.

Other subscribers send messages intended for one person to the whole list, or send messages to a few people which should be sent to the whole list. If you are replying to one member with a message intended just for them, do it in a separate e-mail directed to that person only. Conversely, if you have a question or comment of general applicability, don't send it to a small subset of the members. Post it to the threaded discussion so that all can learn from it and respond to it.

A common problem is including long URLs which wrap across lines and thus may not work when the recipients attempt to click on the link. If the URL you wish to include is long, convert it to a short one using a service such as http://tinyurl.com/. If you are including a link to a book on Amazon.com, simplify the URL. For example, http://www.amazon.com/BIONIC-eTeamwork-Jaclyn-Kostner/dp/0793148340/sr=1-2/qid=1161548786/ref=sr_1_2/002-3820744-1399236?ie=UTF8&s=books can be reduced to http://www.amazon.com/dp/0793148340 by removing the title text and all characters after the product number.

Many of the tools listed under Team Spaces also provide threaded discussion capability. For a separate tool, applications such as UBB.threads at http://www.ubbcentral.com/ can be obtained inexpensively, installed, and integrated with the intranet and other collaboration tools.

For public threaded discussion tools available on the Internet, see:

- Google Groups at http://groups.google.com/
- MSN Groups at http://groups.msn.com/
- Yahoo! Groups at http://groups.yahoo.com/

Expertise locators and ask the expert

Systems for finding experts on particular subjects, allowing individuals to enter details about what they know and can do, and others to search for all people having desired skills, experience, or knowledge; and systems for asking questions of experts and obtaining the answers.

Connecting people so that they can take advantage of the expertise of others is one of the desired modes of knowledge flow in a typical KM programme. This can be accomplished in several ways. The organisation may be structured by expertise, and if so, the manager of a group of specialists in a specific topic can be contacted with a request for help from that group. Communities of practice span organisational structures to bring together subject-matter experts, and can be tapped for expertise.

Another common method is to create a database of all experts in the organisation which can be searched to find those with required expertise. Such tools are usually called skills inventories, expertise locators, or electronic yellow page systems. The challenge with such systems is to encourage employees to enter and maintain their personal data. Even with mandates from top management to do so, many people do not enjoy this task. As a result, they enter minimal information and don't keep it updated as they develop new skills.

Information entered in a skills database can include technical knowledge, process expertise, work experience, languages spoken, roles performed, customer and industry experience, community membership, professional organisations, publications, certifications, and so forth. The more details collected, the more can be searched for, but at the cost of complexity and possibly annoying the users who must rate themselves on a multitude of categories.

Social software (see p115) can help address the challenge of motivating employees to maintain their expertise in a tool. By allowing users to define their own tags for both interests and skills, a folksonomy of expertise can be developed which is less onerous than a massive list of standard skills. If a social networking tool offers other desirable features such as photos, personalised information, and friends, it may draw in users who will also enter and maintain their skills.

Some software vendors offer tools for expertise management which purport to automatically identify experts in the organisation based on the content of their e-mail messages, web pages visited, documents viewed, and other online activities. Such tools may raise concerns about personal privacy, and their effectiveness is subject to debate. Expertise management tools include:

- AskMe http://www.askmecorp.com/
- Autonomy Collaboration and Expertise Networks http://www.autonomy.com/content/Products/CEN/
- OutStart Participate http://www.outstart.com/

■ Tacit http://www.tacit.com/

A process to allow users to ask the expert can be implemented in several ways. It can be done by tapping into a skills inventory or expertise management tool. A standalone tool which allows users to enter questions, routes these to designated experts, and returns answers which are also captured in a database can be developed or obtained.

Another technique is to use existing threaded discussions to reach experts within communities who can reply to questions. This is a typical use of threaded discussions anyway, so adding this capability is simple. To do so, ask the moderator to designate at least two subscribers who are assigned as experts who monitor the threaded discussion. The moderator is usually one of these experts. At least one expert should be on duty every work day. Users can be told to expect an e-mail response within 48 hours with one of the following: the answer to their question, the status of the expert's search for the answer and when to expect it, or a statement that the answer is unlikely to be provided, but may come from other subscribers. If you use this method, you may not need to implement a separate expertise locator tool. Also see:

■ 'Expertise location and the learning organization' by Judith Lamont at http://www.kmworld.com/Articles/ReadArticle.aspx?ArticleID=9410
■ 'Expertise location without technology' by Shawn Callahan at http://www.anecdote.com.au/archives/2006/06/expertise_locat_1.html
■ 'Expertise Management: New Myths and Old Realities' interview with Yogesh Malhotra by Debra D'Agostino at

http://www.kmnetwork.com/Expertise_Management.html

Metadata and tags
Information about information – data fields added to documents, websites, files, or lists which allow related items to be listed, searched for, navigated to, syndicated, and collected.

Metadata allows information to be found through browsing, searching, and other means. It defines the context of the information, how it is classified within a taxonomy, and how it is related to other information. Metadata may be applied automatically based on the origin of the content, assigned by the content owner when submitting it to a repository, or added by a knowledge manager or assistant to ensure it is done properly.

Tags are a form of metadata which can be applied by users to help them retrieve content according to their own view of how it should be categorised. Tags can be applied to web pages, documents, people, photos, music, and any other form of electronic content. These tags can also allow others to find content based on a folksonomy. The problem with a folksonomy as opposed to a taxonomy is that there are no imposed standards, and thus inconsistent tags will likely exist for information which should be tagged uniformly.

Metadata should be based on the standard taxonomy defined for the organisation. It should be embedded in repository entry forms as mandatory fields with pick lists so that contributed content is correctly classified. Search engines should offer the option to search by the available metadata fields so that results will be as specific as possible.

Examples of metadata are customer name, industry, country, product or service, project identifier, technology type, date, revenue amount, etc. Whenever possible, metadata values should be supplied from a table, rather than entered as free-form text in an input field. The reason for this is that if, for example, each user is allowed to enter the customer name, then there will be many variations, and it will be difficult to search by customer name. If one user enters GM and another enters General Motors, the value of metadata is diminished. Offering a pick list containing the standard customer names will avoid this problem. Also see:

- 'Introduction to Metadata: Pathways to Digital Information' by Tony Gill, Anne Gilliland-Swetland, and Murtha Baca at http://www.getty.edu/research/conducting_research/standards/intrometadata/
- Understanding Metadata at http://www.niso.org/standards/resources/UnderstandingMetadata.pdf
- The Semantic Web at http://www.w3.org/2001/sw/
- The Dublin Core Metadata Initiative at http://dublincore.org/
- Metadata.Net at http://metadata.net/
- Taxonomy and Metadata Conference Call Series http://www.earley.com/webinars.htm
- KMWorld Buyers Guide: Content Management http://www.kmworld.com/BuyersGuide/

Search engines

Tools which allow searching for documents, files, list items, content, and answers to questions – allow specifying the scope or domain of the search, whether to search on text or metadata, and how results should be presented. For many users, search is the primary tool they wish to use to find information, answer questions, and learn about a topic. The success of Google Web Search on the Internet has resulted in the widespread expectation that searching within an organisation should work the same way. Users would like to enter just a few words into a search text box and be presented with a list of results which match exactly what they are seeking. Too many hits are not desired, nor are too few, nor are irrelevant ones.

There are significant differences between the quality of results returned by an Internet search and from an intranet search. Page ranking is typically done based on a large sample of links, which works well in the gigantic realm of the Internet, but not as well in the smaller confines of an intranet.

Users should be able to narrow or broaden the types of content, the domains or sites, and the range of metadata values to be included in the search. They should be able to search for text strings, metadata values, or content titles. Familiar syntax such as Boolean operators, quotation marks, and command words used by popular search engines such as Google should be offered. The ability to refine searches, use advanced search functions, and remember previous searches should be provided.

Using the examples of metadata previously provided, a typical metadata search should allow finding content by customer name, industry, country, product or service, project identifier, technology type, date, or revenue amount. For example, search for customer name=Ford, service=consulting, and date>January 1, 2001 and <January 1, 2002. The results should be consulting services sold to Ford in 2001.

A typical text search should allow entering a text string and finding content which contains that string or similar text.

For example, entering 'electric battery' in the search text box should return all content containing that string. Content title search should allow finding files whose title contains a specific text string. For example, searching for '+Honda +Civic +engine' in the content title field should return only documents or photos about Honda Civic engines.

Look for opportunities to integrate existing intranet search with specialised search within the KM environment. If your intranet offers a best bets feature for common searches, take advantage of that by defining best bets for the most frequently searched for topics. If not, consider implementing this feature.

Reviewing the logs of your search engine will allow you to get insight into what users are looking for. You can use this information to supply the most frequently searched for terms in your user interface. You can also use it to improve navigation, offer best bets, and update metadata definitions. Knowledge assistants can monitor user searches to better prepare for user requests. Most intranet, portal, and repository tools include search engines as part of the standard offering. If these don't provide adequate functionality, consider adding a commercial search tool to strengthen the existing environment. See the link to the KMWorld Buyers Guide below. Also see:

- Enterprise Search Center at http://www.enterprisesearchcenter.com/
- Search Engine Watch at http://searchenginewatch.com/
- Search Solutions Jumpstart Conference Call Series http://www.earley.com/webinars.htm
- KMWorld Buyers Guide: Enterprise Search http://www.kmworld.com/BuyersGuide/

Archiving

Offline file storage for legal, audit, or historical purposes, using tapes, CDs, or other long-term media.

As part of the lifecycle of information, archiving is an important final stage. Keeping too much old information available online consumes valuable storage which could be better used for newer information, increases the number of irrelevant search results returned, and adds to the effort required to maintain, migrate, and reclassify content.

There are good reasons to archive content rather than simply delete it. Laws may require content to be kept for specific periods. Internal and external audits may require document retention. Preserving information as a part of history is another worthy goal. There are also times when information which had been thought to be no longer useful later turns out to be needed. Archiving information addresses each of these requirements.

The ideal information lifecycle management process provides an easy method for content to be reviewed, with the reusable content preserved and the other content archived on suitable media. For example, at the end of a project, all documents in the project team space are listed, the user ticks boxes for the reusable ones, and then clicks on an archive button. The result is that the reusable documents are extracted from the team space and stored in the appropriate repository using the associated metadata, and all other documents are archived to a CD which is then stored in the specified archive library. Also see:

- 'Content Life: The Art of Archiving' by Paul Chin at http://www.intranetjournal.com/articles/200405/pij_05_18_04a.html

■ Content Archiving at http://elibrary.
destinationkm.com/rlist/term/Content-
Archiving.html

Blogs

Websites where entries are made (such
as in a journal or diary), displayed in a
reverse chronological order; often provide
commentary or news on a particular subject;
some function as personal online diaries or
logbooks; combine text, images, and links
to other blogs and websites; typically provide
archives in calendar form, local search,
syndication feeds, reader comment posting,
trackback links from other blogs, blogroll links
to other recommended blogs, and categories
of entries tagged for retrieval by topic.

Blogs are a way of empowering
users to express their ideas, record their
thinking, and link to others who are doing
the same. Organisations can use blogs
to communicate, solicit comments, and
engage in online conversations. Blogs serve
as a good archive of communications,
since each entry is stored by date, and it is
possible to search just within a specific blog
to find previous posts.

In 'Naked Conversations' at http://
redcouch.typepad.com/weblog/2005/05/
chapter_2_why_b.html Robert Scoble and
Shel Israel wrote:

"There are six key differences between
blogging and any other communications
channel. These are the Six Pillars of Blogging:

1. Publishable. Anyone can publish
   a blog. You can do it cheaply and
   post often. Each posting is instantly
   available worldwide.
2. Findable. Through search engines,
   people will find blogs by subject, by
   author, or both. The more you post, the
   more findable you become.

3. Social. The blogosphere is one big
   conversation. Interesting topical
   conversations move from site to site,
   linking to each other. Through
   blogs, people with shared interests
   build relationships unrestricted by
   geographic borders.
4. Viral. Information often spreads faster
   through blogs than via a news service.
   No form of viral marketing matches the
   speed and efficiency of a blog.
5. Syndicatable. By clicking on an icon,
   you can get free 'home delivery' of
   RSS-enabled blogs into your e-mail
   software. RSS lets you know when a blog
   you subscribe to is updated, saving you
   search time. This process is considerably
   more efficient than the last-generation
   method of visiting one page of one
   website at a time looking for changes.
6. Linkable. Because each blog can link to
   all others, every blogger has access to
   the tens of millions of people who visit
   the blogosphere every day.

You can find each of these elements
elsewhere. None is, in itself, all that
remarkable. But in final assembly, they
are the benefits of the most powerful
two-way Internet communications tool so
far developed."

For KM, blogs are good tools for
communications, personal KM, and social
networks. As a communications tool, they
are available online, can be easily searched,
and can be syndicated and subscribed
to using RSS or other feeds. For personal
KM, blogs offer a way of keeping a journal
of insights, techniques, pointers, and
contacts. They are the modern version of lab
notebooks, and can be easily shared with
others to allow them to take advantage of
what the blogger has recorded.

For social networks, blogs provide a way to connect those with ideas on related topics. Features typically used in blogs that enable these connections include blogrolls linking to other blogs, comment entry forms to allow others to respond to blog entries, and trackbacks linking to other blogs which reference blog entries.

Blogs can eliminate the need for websites and newsletters, which may be more costly to maintain. Individual departments can each be given their own blogs, which can feature a photo of the department manager and link to the organisation chart. News items can be entered as blog entries, and subscriptions can be offered as RSS feeds. Separate website maintainers and newsletter editors are thus no longer needed.

External blogs offer a way for customers and partners to interact with an organisation. By inviting comments on external blogs and replying to those comments, an organisation can demonstrate its transparency, responsiveness, and customer awareness. It can also receive useful suggestions, timely alerts about problems, and helpful feedback on products and services. Also see:

- *Business Blogs: A Practical Guide* by Bill Ives and Amanda Watlington http://www.amazon.com/dp/0976618001/
- *Naked Conversations: How Blogs are Changing the Way Businesses Talk with Customers* by Robert Scoble and Shel Israel at http://www.amazon.com/dp/047174719X/
- KM bloggers from Wikipedia http://en.wikipedia.org/wiki/KM_bloggers

Wikis

Websites which allow users to easily add, remove, edit, and change most available content – effective for collaborative writing and self-service website creation and maintenance.

A wiki is a website which can be edited by anyone, thus making it easy to collaborate on writing a document, creating a website, or collecting information on a topic. It has been most successfully used in the Wikipedia, a free encyclopedia that has achieved dramatic levels of contribution and use.

Within organisations, wikis have been used to create internal equivalents of the Wikipedia for knowledge about the organisation and its activities. They are very well-suited for the production of documentation by teams of writers and editors, since the shared editing capability is ideal for this task. Wikis are also useful for collecting diverse inputs, links to other sites, and multiple points of view.

Attempts to use wikis for knowledge repositories have been less successful. Whereas the alphabet provides the standard taxonomy for Wikipedia, other taxonomies are more difficult to impose and maintain using wikis. Since anyone can add a new wiki page, it is difficult to control the proliferation of such pages. Text entry in a new wiki page is generally unstructured, which is less desirable than form entry for repositories.

Participation in wikis is another challenge. They are often created by a committed individual who hopes that others will share a similar passion for the topic and add to the content. When these others fail to materialise, the wiki ends up being maintained primarily by the original creator, and thus is more similar to a blog or website.

Wikis can be victimised by vandalism or contentious arguments between opposing factions. In Wikipedia, talk pages are used to discuss an article and to attempt to reach agreement on a neutral end result. Inside an organisation, if disagreement about a topic exists, it could result in content thrashing as the differing viewpoints are alternately restored to prominence.

If you are interested in using wikis as part of a KM programme, pick an application where they fit well, and use a pilot implementation to see how it works. If the application performs acceptably, user participation is good, and the desired results are achieved, it can be expanded to additional users and applications. If not, you can capture the lessons learnt and move on to the next pilot. Here are sources of information to help choose wiki software or a hosting service:

- http://www.wikimatrix.org/wizard.php
- http://en.wikibooks.org/wiki/Wiki_Science:How_to_start_a_Wiki#Free_wiki_hosting
- http://www.fullcirc.com/weblog/2005/04/riomenajang-wiki-resources.htm
- http://en.wikipedia.org/wiki/Comparison_of_wiki_farms
- http://c2.com/cgi/wiki?WikiFarms

Also see:

- Wiki defined in Wikipedia http://en.wikipedia.org/wiki/Wiki
- Wikis: Tools for Information Work And Collaboration by Jane Klobas at http://www.amazon.com/dp/1843341786/
- Booki, the wiki of 'Wikis: Tools for information Work and Collaboration' http://www.booki.info/display/website/Home
- KmWiki a collaborative persistent 'conversation' on all matters related to KM http://kmwiki.wikispaces.com/

Podcasts

Recorded broadcasts which can be listened to online, or downloaded manually or automatically through syndication and then listened to on portable MP3 players at the listener's convenience.

Podcasting is an excellent way to reach an audience which is young, mobile, and prefers listening to reading. Recording a podcast is inexpensive, easy, and fast. Interviews can be recorded over phone lines or using a VoIP (Voice over Internet Protocol) tool such as Skype (http://www.skype.com/). Podcasts can be delivered through several channels. An audio file in MP3 format can be posted for online listening. Syndicated subscriptions can be offered to allow automatic downloading to iPods or other MP3 players. Transcripts can be posted for those who prefer reading to listening.

Many people enjoy the flexibility of being able to listen to podcasts while driving, flying, walking, running, exercising, or engaging in some other activity. The fact that through an RSS subscription a podcast can be automatically delivered without the need for a user to visit a website and take action makes it easy to keep up with a podcast series.

As part of a communications plan, podcasts can be used to introduce a KM programme, keep users updated on progress, and demonstrate ongoing management commitment. Produce interviews with the senior executive, KM team members, and satisfied users to help promote and maintain awareness.

Use storytelling during podcasts to ignite action, implement new ideas, communicate who you are, instill organisational values, foster collaboration, and share knowledge. It's an excellent way for users to share their knowledge verbally without the need to write anything down, submit any documents, or enter any data in forms. The recording and transcript provide explicit instances of the tacit knowledge, and can be reused later.

If you encourage teams to discuss lessons learnt, proven practices, and success stories on podcasts, the knowledge will be more effectively shared than if the same information was written down and submitted to a database. Look for ways to persuade people to talk about what they know, and others will be able to take advantage. A regular podcast series with a brand name, logo, website, theme music, and host can be a very effective element in a KM programme. Also see:

- Podcasting Tools http://www.podcasting-tools.com/
- Books on podcasting at http://www.amazon.com/s/ref=nb_ss_gw/?url=search-alias%3Daps&field-keywords=podcasting

Syndication and aggregation

Using feeds available from a website to provide an updated list of its content in the form of a subscription, an embedded portion of a website, or a collection of disparate content on a particular topic – typically uses RSS or Atom syndication and .rss, .xml, or .rdf files for the feeds. Syndication is a way of providing content such that it can be subscribed to using a feed reader, integrated into a website as a subset of that site, or aggregated with similar content. Aggregation is a way of collecting multiple syndicated feeds into a single feed or as part of a unified website.

You can use syndication in a variety of ways. Blogs can be aggregated into a common site showing the latest entries from all blog sources. Subscriptions to blogs and podcasts can be offered. The latest updates made to a wiki can be provided as a feed.

The ongoing results of predefined searches can be displayed. Threaded discussions can be tracked through a feed reader, and the latest posts can be displayed as news items on a community website.

Syndicated content can be used in many ways, including being fed to standalone readers, embedded in web browsers or e-mail clients, integrated with personalised websites such as My Yahoo!, and delivered as e-mail messages. It can also be aggregated on websites. Here are three examples of aggregation of blog content:

- Blogdigger http://www.blogdigger.com/
- Technorati http://www.technorati.com/
- topix.net http://www.topix.net/blogs

Also see:

- Feed 101 http://www.feedburner.com/fb/a/aboutrss
- 'What Are Syndication Feeds' by Shelley Powers http://www.oreilly.com/catalog/syndicationfeeds/
- Books on RSS at http://www.amazon.com/s/ref=nb_ss_gw/?url=search-alias%3Daps&field-keywords=rss

Social software

A range of tools which facilitate social networking, typically personal web pages including bios, photos, interests, audio and video, links to friends, messages from friends, and personal networks; often referred to as Web 2.0 to include a broad range of tools such as blogs, wikis, and RSS feeds.

Social networking sites such as MySpace for teenagers and musicians, Facebook for college students and alumni, and LinkdIn and openBC for business people have been rapidly increasing their numbers of users.

Given the popularity of these sites, it may be possible to capture some of this user enthusiasm within an organisation by providing similar functionality. Consider offering users the ability to easily create their own personal home pages. As part of these pages, extract as much information as is already available from other databases, such as basic employee information (e-mail address, instant messaging ID, office location, phone numbers, skills, etc.). If the user has a blog, integrate it using syndication.

Allow users to enter their biographies and personal statements, upload their photos, add links to favourite sites, declare interests and expertise, and add friends in their social network. Integrate feeds from other systems, including the team spaces belonged to, latest threaded discussion posts, point totals from the incentive points system, courses attended and enrolled in, and contributions made to knowledge repositories.

If you make the site fun, attractive, and voluntary, it may become very popular and spread in viral fashion. If this is the case, then whatever you embed in the tool will have widespread visibility. Make sure that all embedded features are for the benefit of the users, to avoid the appearance of the equivalence of advertising. Give the users something that they enjoy using, and the organisation can benefit from the byproducts – improved communications, social networking, and expertise location. Also see:

- List of social networking websites from Wikipedia http://en.wikipedia.org/wiki/List_of_social_networking_websites
- LinkedIn https://www.linkedin.com/home
- openBC https://www.openbc.com/
- Facebook http://www.facebook.com/
- MySpace http://www.myspace.com/

External access

Capability for users outside of a company's firewall to have access to selected websites and team spaces to allow collaboration with retirees, partners, and customers who would otherwise be blocked from the company's internal network – requires technical, security, and legal elements.

In *The Wealth of Knowledge: Intellectual Capital and the Twenty-first Century Organization* (http://www.amazon.com/dp//0385500726/) by Thomas Stewart, in Chapter 5, pp 85—87, the following key elements of a KM programme are defined based on the experience of Steve Denning at the World Bank:

1. communities of practice;
2. place (online presence for the communities);
3. help desk;
4. Yellow Pages (who-knows-what directory);
5. primer (FAQ);
6. knowledge artifacts (records of previous projects, emphasising best practices and lessons learnt);
7. bulletin board;
8. doorway (a provision for outside access).

The final item, doorway, is often overlooked as an enabler for knowledge sharing to occur. Here are three examples of why external access can be valuable to an organisation.

There is increasing concern about the loss of valuable knowledge as the workforce ages and the baby boomers retire. Many of these retirees are willing to continue to share the knowledge they have gained over many years of experience. In order to do so, they need to be given access to community tools such as portals, team spaces, and threaded discussions. Providing this access poses minimal security risks and offers great benefits in ongoing contributions from the most experienced community members.

Partners need access to similar information to the internal sales force in order to effectively sell and deliver products and services as part of the partnership. Giving them access to the relevant knowledge bases, under appropriate nondisclosure agreements, will greatly enhance the success of the partnership. And partners can contribute their knowledge to communities within the organisation if they are allowed to do so.

Customers may also be able to share knowledge as extended community members. They can also benefit from having access to problem resolution knowledge bases so they can solve their own problems, product information databases so they can buy more products, and logistics and support tracking systems so they can stay current on the status of pending deliveries and services without the need to contact a call centre. For projects being delivered to customers, it is very beneficial to include them as participants in the team spaces for their projects.

Dealing with each of these opportunities in a way which maintains required levels of security, protects intellectual property, and enables the right level of access can be tricky. But it is worth creating the people, process, and technology mechanisms to make it work. The technology elements include providing gateways, secure servers, and identity management hardware and software.

Workflow applications

Software which connects and sequences different applications, components, and people, all of which must be involved in the processing of data to complete an instance of a process.

Workflow automation is not strictly a knowledge management application, but it can be an important enabler by means of allowing knowledge capture and reuse to be embedded in routine business processes. By so doing, the likelihood of desired knowledge being collected and retrieved at the appropriate times is significantly increased, since there is no separate KM process which may or may not be followed.

For example, for call centres, KCS (Knowledge-Centered Support http://www.serviceinnovation.org/included/docs/library/programs/kcs_brief.pdf) lists Seven Points of Elegance, the first of which is "Capture in the workflow – context and content are captured as the problem is being solved, when the support agent/analyst hangs up the phone there is a reusable solution in the knowledge base. This solution is immediately available to other agents/analysts who have similar context. There is no post call knowledge engineering on the solution (this is what drives the economics of KCS methods). Solutions are reviewed based on demand (reuse)."

Look for opportunities to add knowledge capture and reuse to existing workflow applications, and consider implementing new ones which do this. The result will be fewer extra steps, more automated knowledge flow, and improved business results. Also see:

- KMWorld Buyers Guide: Workflow http://www.kmworld.com/BuyersGuide/
- Books on workflow applications at http://www.amazon.com/s/ref=nb_ss_gw/?url=search-alias%3Daps&field-keywords=%22workflow+applications%22

Process automation applications

Tools which automate previously manual processes, such as the production of proposals, creation of presentations, or the design of products.

Many business processes have been automated with commercially-available or custom applications. Those which are knowledge intensive can be considered for inclusion or integration with a KM initiative. Three examples are proposals, presentations, and product development.

In proposal production, much of the content is standard boilerplate and can be reused as it is on each proposal. Some content must be modified slightly, but is typically included. And some content is unique to the particular opportunity and must be tailored extensively. A proposal automation tool can help streamline the effort required, allowing most of the time to be spent on the custom content, and creating a consistent and appealing format.

Presentations are similar in that they combine slides reused from the past, modified slides, and new slides. There are often problems with inconsistent formats, outdated information, and missing content. A presentation creation tool manages slide content in a library, ensures that the latest versions are used, and enables useful features such as synchronised audio recording. This allows presentations to be delivered as recorded slideshows, which can be used for training and to ensure the highest quality of narration.

The University of Michigan's PLM Development Consortium defines Product Lifecycle Management (PLM) as "an integrated, information-driven approach to all aspects of a product's life – from its design inception through its manufacture, deployment and maintenance, culminating in its removal from service and final disposal". In 'Defining PLM' at http://www.ugs.com/about_us/facts_philosophy/define_plm.shtml UGS states "PLM could

be defined as an information strategy. It builds a coherent data structure, consolidating systems. Or, you could call PLM an enterprise strategy. It lets global organisations innovate, develop, support and retire products as one company, while capturing best practices and lessons learnt along the way. At UGS, we view PLM as at once an information strategy, an enterprise strategy and ultimately a transformational business strategy. We see it as a comprehensive approach to innovation built on enterprise-wide access to a common repository of product information and processes."

These and other knowledge-based business processes should be reviewed and considered for inclusion in your KM programme. Some will be too big on their own, but some will fit well with other KM components and can be tied in as appropriate. Also see:

- Pragmatech Proposal Automation Suite http://www.pragmatech.com/ProductsAndSolutions/SolutionsByProduct/ProposalAutomationSuite.aspx
- Avitage PowerPoint Management http://www.avitage.com/offerings_ppm.asp
- HP Product Lifecycle Management http://h71028.www7.hp.com/enterprise/cache/8861-0-0-225-121.html

E-learning

Tools which enable the delivery and tracking of online training courses.

Learning is one of the basic activities of KM. Organisations usually have a Learning and Development function as part of Human Resources, and it is responsible for a wide range of employee development, including classroom instruction and online learning. KM programmes sometimes report into this function with the goal of better integrating knowledge reuse with learning.

E-learning is important to a KM initiative in several ways. KM training is an important people component, and e-learning can be used to deliver it. Integrating content from knowledge repositories into e-learning can improve its effectiveness. Delivering e-learning along with knowledge content returned through searches or through browsing can enhance the usefulness of the results and better leverage training content. Tracking training which employees have taken can help suggest new offerings they should consider as part of a specific knowledge requirement and as part of their ongoing development.

If your KM programme is part of the Learning and Development function, then you will have strong incentives to tightly couple the two environments. If not, then look for opportunities to establish ties to that function, and explore possible points of integration which will be mutually beneficial. At a minimum, provide a link to the organisation's e-learning tool as part of the standard navigation bar in the KM user interface. Also see:

- Elearnspace: everything elearning http://www.elearnspace.org/
- The eLearning Guild http://www.elearningguild.com/
- Books on e-learning at http://www.amazon.com/s/ref=nb_ss_gw/?url=search-alias%3Daps&field-keywords=elearning

Subscription management

Tools which allow content providers to reach subscribers on an opt-in basis, and subscribers to sign up to receive periodicals and other communications based on their interests.

In addition to the rapidly emerging use of RSS feeds for subscribing to syndicated content such as blogs and podcasts, there is still a need for allowing people to subscribe to traditional newsletters. Users do not appreciate receiving e-mail which they did not request, and if they continue to receive unwanted distributions, they will most likely delete them unread, or set mailbox rules to do so automatically.

To avoid having your newsletter regarded as spam, provide a tool which allows those who do wish to receive it to voluntarily subscribe. By automating this process, you can reduce the time spent manually adding and deleting names from a distribution list, automatically handle bounced messages, and quickly determine how many subscribers you have.

When a newsletter is first created, you can send out a one-time announcement to a broad distribution list of everyone in the organisation offering a sample issue, inviting them to subscribe, and telling them how to simply do so. But after doing this once, avoid doing it again to prevent annoying the recipients. Provide prominent links to the subscription page from your key websites. Include clear instructions in each issue on how to subscribe and unsubscribe. If an issue is forwarded from a current subscriber to a colleague, it should be obvious to that colleague how to subscribe. If a subscriber decides they no longer want to receive your newsletter, don't make it difficult to unsubscribe.

In addition to the ability to subscribe to specific periodicals, you may wish to allow subscription to topics. In that way, if additional newsletters are created for an existing topic, they can be sent to those people who have already expressed an interest in the subject. Other forms of subscription include RSS feeds, threaded discussions through e-mail, and content alerts. Alerts are e-mail messages sent to team space, portal, or repository users to let them know that new content has been posted. Remind your users of all of these subscription options and help them to take advantage of each method for their specific needs. Also see:

- Google Alerts
  http://www.google.com/alerts
- Yahoo! Alerts http://alerts.yahoo.com/
- Managing Alerts (Windows SharePoint Services) http://www.microsoft.com/resources/documentation/wss/2/all/adminguide/en-us/stsf13.mspx?mfr=true

Incentive points tracking

Systems for awarding and tracking points for desired knowledge management behaviours, both automatically as triggered by events and manually through forms entry.

Recognition for contributing, reusing, and sharing knowledge can help encourage people to continue to do so. Financial or other tangible rewards can be used in conjunction with recognition, but are not necessarily required to motivate the desired behaviours.

HP's IT Resource Center (ITRC) forums at http://forums.itrc.hp.com/cm/1,,,00.html are a good example of using a points tracking system to recognise those who share their knowledge. This is the gathering place for IT Professionals to solve problems, exchange ideas, and learn lessons from fellow peers who also use the IT Resource Center. HP engineers participate in all of these forums to share their advice, but these forums are intended as a peer-to-peer resource.

The 'Submit Points' option allows members to rate replies to their questions by assigning points to those members who provide replies or solutions to problems. On the website, the Top 25 members and the Top Ten new members are listed prominently, and this helps encourage members to help each other and award points as a result.

An example of a commercially-available tool is Enterprise Knowledge Incentives (EKI), Knexa's proprietary reward system for knowledge sharing (http://www.knexa.com/features.shtml). "EKI imbeds into knowledge sharing technologies a specialised reward and recognition system that awards a score for activities ranging from contributing documents to answering questions posed by other employees. It provides a sophisticated way to track, measure and reward myriad knowledge sharing activities."

You can also develop your own web-based application to keep track of KM points. These points can be earned by contributing reusable content to an approved knowledge repository that is later reused by others, reusing content from an approved knowledge repository and submitting user feedback for that content, or assisting in a KM initiative approved by a member of the KM team. KM initiative activities can include regularly answering questions in a threaded discussion, serving as an 'ask the expert' contact, actively moderating a threaded discussion, presenting on a community call or at a community event, participating in a pilot, or any thing else that helps the KM programme to succeed.

In order to receive points for contribution, all required metadata must be completed as part of the submission. In order to receive points for reuse, user feedback must be submitted rating the usefulness of the reusable content and estimating the dollar impact of the reuse. Submission of this feedback will trigger points being credited to both the user and the original contributor. The higher the usefulness rating, the more points that will be awarded to the original contributor.

These ideas give you a starting point for designing your own system. You can choose to include any or all of these concepts, or think of others which are more suitable for your organisation. The key is to try something simple to see if it works. You can try giving financial rewards to those who earn the most points, or recognise them in some other way. Publishing the leaders on the KM home page, in newsletters, and in special messages from the senior executive will help reinforce the importance of the programme, spur a friendly competition between users, and recognise those who excel.

Survey and metrics reporting automation

Systems for conducting, collecting, and publishing survey data; and systems for collecting, distributing, and publishing data on key performance metrics.

If you will be using surveys to understand user needs and satisfaction, and if you plan to report on metrics, you will need tools to support these activities. Automated survey administration, data collection and compilation, and report publishing will make it easier to do this regularly. Applications to prepare monthly metrics reports with a minimum of human intervention will allow the members of the KM team to spend their time on tasks more worthy of their skills.

If automation of these two processes is not possible, reconsider whether they are worth doing. Survey and metrics data provided with a minimum of effort through automated systems can be put to productive use. But if you find that the limited staff

members are consumed for days at a time each month to produce reports, figure out a simpler way. This serves as a good reminder for all technology components. They should support people and processes, and not detract from them. Technology is a means to and end, not the end itself.

Summary

The technology options available to support KM continue to expand. Vendors promote their offerings with promises to solve all current and future knowledge-related challenges. A healthy dose of skepticism is required to sort through the various claims.

Keeping in mind the need to balance technology with the people and process components, there is still a very important role for technology in enabling knowledge to flow. The user interface is frequently through the intranet and provides access to the other components. Team spaces and virtual meeting rooms support collaboration and communities. Portals and repositories provide storage and retrieval of reusable content. Threaded discussions and expertise locators allow people to connect. Metadata and tags enable search engines to find useful content, which is preserved through archiving.

Blogs, wikis, podcasts, syndication, aggregation, and social networking software are all part of the emerging Web 2.0 portfolio of social software which is democratising knowledge and connecting people. External access allows retirees, partners, and customers to engage with members of the organisation in useful ways. Workflow applications and process automation applications embed knowledge sharing in the routine operations of a business.

E-learning allows users to learn at their convenience and at the time of need.

Subscription management provides a
way to opt in to regularly receive desired
information. An incentive points tracking
system helps recognise those people who
demonstrate the desired behaviours. Survey
and metrics reporting automation allows
the organisation to monitor how its KM
programme is performing and to make any
needed adjustments.

Chapter 10: Communities – Creating, building and sustaining them

Communities are fundamental to connecting people with related interests so that they can learn together, share with one another, reuse each other's ideas, collaborate, and innovate. Starting a community is an excellent first step in launching a KM initiative, and can be used as a building block for more elaborate functionality.

Communities are groups of people who share an interest, a specialty, a role, a concern, a set of problems, or a passion for a specific topic. Community members deepen their understanding by interacting on an ongoing basis, asking and answering questions, sharing their knowledge, reusing good ideas, and solving problems for one another.

Communities enable knowledge to flow between people. Community members:

- Learn from other members of the community; from invited guest speakers about successes, failures, case studies, and new trends; and through mentoring.
- Share new ideas, lessons learnt, proven practices, insights, and practical suggestions.
- Reuse solutions through asking and answering questions, applying shared insights, and retrieving posted material.
- Collaborate through threaded discussions, conversations, and interactions.
- Innovate through brainstorming, building on each other's ideas, and keeping informed on emerging developments.

Richard McDermott, an authority on communities, states that "healthy communities have a driving purpose, clear activities, a sense of accomplishment, and high management expectations. The heart of a community of practice includes peer-to-peer relationships, responsibility for stewarding a body of knowledge, membership which crosses boundaries, and room for dealing with whatever comes up."

Communities come in two main varieties. Communities of Practice have a rich and formal set of activities, governance, and structure and are based on common roles or specialties. Communities of Interest are for topics that don't require a lot of formal structure but need threaded discussions for collaboration and knowledge sharing.

Communities of Practice have members with a particular work role or expertise. These communities are focused on developing expertise, skills, and proficiency in the specialty. The motivation is to master the discipline, learn about the specialty, and solve problems together. An example of a role-based community is project management, and an example of an expertise-based community is Microsoft SharePoint.

Communities of Interest are loosely connected groups of people who want to learn about a particular topic. They make no commitment to deliver something together. The motivation is to stay current on the topic and to be able to ask and answer questions about it. An example is all people who have an interest in KM, even if they have jobs which are not KM-specific.

Getting started

The first thing to do is to decide what topic you wish to address in a community. Pick a compelling topic that will be of interest to many people in your organisation. The potential members must be passionate about the subject for collaboration, and it must be relevant to their work.

Before creating a new community, check to see if there is an existing community already focused on the proposed topic or on related one. If nothing similar already exists, then you can proceed to create a new one. If communities already exist in your organisation, then answer the following questions.

Is your topic already covered as part of another community? If so, offer to help the leader of that community. Help can include increasing membership, booking speakers, leading calls and meetings, responding to questions, and sharing useful information.

Is there an existing community focused on a related topic? If so, approach its leader about expanding it to include your topic. This helps achieve critical mass, broadens the appeal of the community, and provides the same type of help as mentioned above.

Is there an old community that is inactive but could be resurrected or migrated to form the new community? If so, ask if you can take over the leadership, or harvest the membership list to start the new one. Reusing existing membership lists, community tools, and knowledge content can save time in starting a new community. If the answers to all of these questions are negative, then you can create a new community for the desired topic. The subsequent sections provide the steps to follow.

Select a community leader

You need committed leaders for communities. Community leaders should know the subject in depth, have energy for stimulating collaboration among the members, and be able to devote sufficient time to leadership activities. These activities include regularly spending time increasing membership, lining up speakers, hosting calls and meetings, asking and answering questions, and posting information which is useful to the members.

In an actKM discussion on the role of community managers summarised by Arthur Shelley at http://www.actkm.org/userfiles/File/articles/Community_Manager_Role%20ACTKM.pdf, the following attributes were supplied by the participants. Arthur Shelley of Cadbury Schweppes:

"Community manager key responsibilities:

- Lead the community, engage membership and other stakeholders.
- Organise community interactions and activities on a regular basis.
- Ensure the purpose of the community remains aligned with personal aspirations of the members as well as business goals.
- Create an identity for the community to which people want to belong.
- Generate an atmosphere of fun to keep the interactions vibrant.
- Network with potential new community members to promote community benefits.
- Collate feedback from members and facilitate responses to source of feedback.
- Ensure collaboration activities are beneficial to the community members.
- Engage members and generate a sense of commitment to community activities.
- Network with HR and Communications personnel, advise them of interest stories.
- Communicate community benefits and successes to wider stakeholder groups.
- Establish (with members) agreed processes for community activities and events.

- Establish accountabilities and timeframes for agreed projects, tasks and activities.
- Identify objectives, roles and responsibilities for community members.
- Designate resources requirements and determine any funding arrangements.
- Anticipate risks and explore impacts of non-delivery of desired outcomes.
- Establish a monitoring and review process.
- Liaise with the Content Manager to discuss layout and formats of content on the portal.
- Screen submitted content for appropriateness and relevance.
- Encourage members to load useful content to the relevant portal pages."

Shawn Callahan of Anecdote: "Here are the character traits I think a community coordinator should have:

- Well respected.
- Knowledgeable about the community's domain (but not an expert).
- Well connected to a range of community members.
- Keen to develop the community's practice.
- Good communicators.
- Personally interested in community leadership.
- Good workshop and meeting facilitator.
- Likeable.

The other critical feature is that the coordinator should be approved/accepted/chosen by the community leadership."

David Smith of Halliburton: "Our community facilitators:

- Act as the intermediary between people seeking knowledge and people who can provide the knowledge. They actually

seek out experts to support community requests for assistance.
- Identify, maintain and make accessible the collection of knowledge sources in their area of responsibility.
- Facilitate validation of knowledge before updating repository.
- Monitor other Knowledge Communities and other reporting systems to extract new knowledge or identify issues that require solutions.
- Identify needs for new knowledge and stimulate its creation.
- Assist management in prioritising new technology developments based on community needs.
- Manage the community portal.

Facilitator competencies:

- Recognised by peers as competent in broad range of community subjects.
- Good people skills.
- Passionately interested in the community subject area.
- Proficient in KM process and tools."

Matt Moore of Oracle: "Some community coordinator attributes:

- **Passionate** about the domain and the development of a community.
- A **practitioner** of the domain themselves.
- Respected and liked by their **peers**.
- Aware and prepared for the organisational **politics** they will encounter.
- Skilled in facilitation **process** (be it virtual or real).
- Willing to **persevere** on this for months rather than days."

Build community membership

The community will need a critical mass of members. You usually need at least 50 members, with 100 being a better target. A community benefits from a broad range of perspectives. If it has only a small number of like-minded members, it is unlikely that innovative ideas, lively debates, and breakthrough thinking will result. Only 20% or fewer of the members will usually be active in discussions and presentations. In small communities, only a handful of people will speak up, and that will not usually sustain momentum.

The larger the membership, the more likely that any question posed to the community will be answered. By including as much of the available expertise as possible in the community, its ability to respond increases accordingly.

Increasing the size of a community yields more potential speakers at community events and conference calls. It results in greater leverage, since for the same effort, more people realise the benefits. And it helps more people to become comfortable in the community model, which can lead them to join other communities, recruit new members, and launch related communities of interest. To build membership, try to take advantage of existing networks. Is there an existing team that could become the core of a new community? For example, is there a team whose mission aligns with the topic for the new community? If so, these can be the initial members.

Is there an existing distribution list of people interested in the topic? If so, use that list to invite people to join your community. You can also use this list to add subscribers to a threaded discussion. Send a message to the members when you have done this, explaining why this was done, the benefits of the community, and how to unsubscribe if they don't want to belong. After adding these new members, be sure that some useful posts are made to demonstrate the value of remaining subscribed to the threaded discussion.

Skills inventories and expertise locators can be mined to find potential members. Look for people who have declared a specialty, expertise, or an interest in the topic, and invite them to join the community or subscribe them to the threaded discussion. If you are conducting user surveys about other aspects of the KM initiative, you can include questions about topics of interest and communities which users would like to join. Use the results of such surveys to invite members to join associated communities.

Social Network Analysis (see Chapter 8) can be used to identify people who are linked but who may not be part of a formal community. These people can be invited join the community or subscribed to the threaded discussion. After new members are added to the community, you should periodically ask them to help recruit others. Potential members can be invited to attend events to see if they would like to join, subscribe to the threaded discussion, or review community content for possible use.

Publicise the community

Once your community is established, publicise its existence to help recruit new members. This is an ongoing requirement, because new people will join the organisation and need to be informed for the first time, and other people need repeated communications for your message to reach them and to sink in. Write and submit articles to existing newsletters that reach your target audience. Provide a concise description of the community, including its purpose, benefits, events, and tools. Supply an easy-to-use link to follow for more information and to join the community.

Solicit success stories of how the community has helped its members and the organisation to achieve their goals. Publicise these stories within the community and through articles in various publications and websites. Use existing networks to inform possible members about your community. Distribution lists, expertise locators, and other communities can be used to contact potential members through e-mail to make them aware of the community and how to join. Or you can speak at a meeting or on a conference call to solicit new members.

Send a one-time broadcast message to the entire population containing your target audience. Make sure your message is brief, compelling, and visually appealing. Include links to key community sites and, for new members, links allowing them to join. Request that a link to your community be added on all relevant websites. Examples include the intranet home page for your organisation, other community sites, master community directories, related links pages, and other intranet pages related to the community topic. The provided link should go to a page which quickly grabs the interest of the user, shows them the available resources, succinctly describes the benefits, and makes it easy to join the community.

Offer an incentive to join the community. For example, a member will be chosen at random to receive a book about the community topic. Or the 100th member will receive an MP3 player to use to subscribe to the community's podcast. Or everyone who joins receives a complimentary subscription to a relevant industry periodical. You can also recognise existing community members who recruit the most new members. Try all of these tactics, and keep track of which ones yield the best results. Periodically repeat each one.

Keep the community active

Many communities fail because after the effort to create them wanes, there is limited effort devoted to sustaining activity. Help the community thrive by regularly using a variety of interventions.

Hold a regular conference call with a scheduled speaker. The community can decide the desired frequency, but it should be often enough to keep the event in the minds of the members. Speakers can be from within or outside the community. Member speakers can share their experiences and insights. External speakers can be thought leaders, members of other organisations with diverse perspectives, or experts on topics of interest. Speakers can give presentations, lead discussions, or demonstrate concepts. Topics can include proven practices, success stories, lessons learnt from failure, emerging concepts, controversial ideas, tips, techniques, insights, and methods.

Hold periodic events such as face-to-face meetings and training sessions. Meeting in person at least occasionally is essential to building trust. Members who have met, socialised, and learnt about each other's personal interests will have a much easier time collaborating thereafter. Spending more time together than is available on recurring conference calls allows for deeper learning to occur.

Post at least once a week to the community's threaded discussion. Include a summary of a community event, a useful link, or a thought-provoking topic to stimulate discussion. By doing this, you will keep the community at the forefront of the mind of the members. To those browsing the community tools to see if they wish to join, frequent posts serve as an indicator of community health. Some members will typically respond to your posts and useful discussions will ensue.

Look for relevant discussions that are taking place in e-mail exchanges, public distribution lists, or outside of your organisation. Then redirect those discussions to your threaded discussion, copy or link to the key points, or summarise the highlights. By drawing these external discussions into your community, you will provide useful insights, demonstrate the value of membership, and possibly attract new members.

Regularly suggest to those with questions or interest in your topic that they join your community and use its tools. These people may surface in multiple ways. They may send you a question or call you with a problem. Or they might contact the knowledge assistants looking for help. Or someone who knows of your expertise in the topic may refer someone else to you, either by forwarding an e-mail message or by providing your name and phone number. However the question or interest is identified, it represents an excellent opportunity to make the initiator aware of the community and use the community to respond. This builds credibility, adds new members, and creates value for the organisation.

As already mentioned, only 20% or fewer of the members will usually be active in discussions and presentations. The other 80% are often referred to as lurkers. Lurking is okay, because it allows those members who are new, inexperienced, or shy to learn from the more active members. Lurkers play an important role in communities as the beneficiaries of much of what is being discussed by others. They can benefit from seeing how others solved problems, listening to speakers, and reading posted materials. So while active members are essential to a community's success, so are silent ones.

Provide community tools
To enable the community to collaborate, offer one or more tools for members to use. People make up the community, and

tools support collaboration among the members. A collaborative team space can be used for document sharing, meetings, lists, polls, photos, and schedules. Instead of using e-mail to send meeting reminders, presentation files, and minutes, these can all be posted to the community team space and thus save network bandwidth and inbox capacity. Documents and files intended for the community should be posted here. Schedules and agendas for meetings, including dial-in instructions, presentation materials, attendees, minutes, and links to recordings can be provided. Community polls on governance issues, opinions, and member feedback can be conducted and summarised. A community roster can be provided for self-maintenance, including photos, profiles, and links. An example of a community team space is Com-Prac at http://groups.yahoo.com/group/com-prac/.

A listing should be added to the organisation's community directory to increase awareness. If a community directory does not already exist, offer to create one. Otherwise, submit a description of your community, a link to its website, and a link for joining. If categories or tags are available, provide all relevant metadata so potential members will be able to search or browse to find your community's topic. An example of a community directory is Google Groups at http://groups.google.com/groups/dir.

Distribution lists are useful for announcements and other push e-mails. Use these for sending out periodic newsletters, one-time announcements, and any other communications which don't need to be archived and aren't likely to prompt discussion. An example of topic-specific distribution lists is Line56 Media's e-newsletters at http://www.line56.com/subscribe/.

A threaded discussion for collaboration should be provided. This is where questions can be asked and answered, ideas can be shared, links to posted documents can be communicated, and an archive of discussions can be preserved and searched. This is a key tool for any community. An example of a community threaded discussion is the actKM discussion List at http://actkm. org/mailman/listinfo/actkm_actkm.org.

Websites can provide information to potential members. Details on the community's topic, leaders, members, events, and links to other resources should be included. Of particular importance, it should offer an obvious and easy-to-use way to join the community, through a single click if at all possible. An example of a community website is the Association of Knowledgework at http:// www.kwork.org/index.html.

Portals or repositories can provide structured content if there is sufficient quantity to warrant such a tool. For those communities with a significant amount of contributed documents, storing it in a portal or repository with rich metadata tagging, search, and alternate viewing capabilities will be worthwhile. For other communities, this will not be needed, and a team space or website will be sufficient. An example of a community portal is KnowledgeBoard at http://www. knowledgeboard.com/index.html.

Wikis enable collaboration on shared documents and content. If the community wishes to capture a body of knowledge which will be evolving and involve iterative definitions from multiple members, a wiki is well-suited to this. An example of a community wiki is KmWiki at http://kmwiki. wikispaces.com/. Blogs are good for communicating when there is a need for permanent links, comments, or trackback

for posted entries. A blog provides a chronological archive which can easily be searched. An example of a community blog is KM Chicago at http://kmchicago. blogspot.com/.

Newsletters communicate community news, facilitate knowledge sharing, and help recruit new members. They can be helpful in reminding members of upcoming events, linking to posted materials, and including articles of interest to members. An example of a community newsletter is the Gurteen Knowledge Letter at http://www. gurteen.com/gurteen/gurteen.nsf/(Views)/ WebNewsList?OpenDocument&Count=9 99. Community conference calls can be recorded, with the consent of the members, and the recordings made available through the community team space, website, or portal. An example of a community conference call is the monthly call of the Community of Consulting and Systems Integration KM Leaders at http://groups. yahoo.com/group/sikmleaders/.

Sustain the community

After a community has been created and developed, it must be nurtured carefully so that it doesn't stagnate or die. Here are some practical tips for how to sustain communities. Don't let a few members dominate. Encourage lurkers when they surface with an occasional post. Invite a variety of members to speak during calls and meetings. Publicise contributions from all members.

Avoid parochialism. Local organisations tend to think of creating local communities and sharing within them, but are reluctant to expand to a global community. Encourage communities to be broader and to include other countries, other parts of the organisation, customers, partners, and former employees. This may be hard to sell, even though wider membership will probably make the communities more successful by supplying more answers to questions, additional perspectives, and more varied experience.

Meet in person, either in a periodic community meeting, or as part of another meeting or training session. Colleagues who see each other regularly are more likely to ask one another for help and to trust one another enough to share documents and other content. Someone who works in the cube next another person will be likely to visit that colleague to ask for help, to bounce ideas off them, or to ask if they have a document that they can use. They are much less likely to post to a threaded discussion or to contact someone they don't know personally. Face-to-face meetings help overcome this challenge by introducing members to one another.

Aim for a variety of speakers, topics, and activities. In community events, don't always have a presentation. Sometimes schedule a field trip, a discussion, or a social event. Invite outside speakers who hold the attention of the audience. Introduce new topics into threaded discussions. Inject humour and levity to keep things light.

Add an ask the expert process for the community. A specific way to use threaded discussions effectively is to ensure posted questions are answered. This is a service level agreement associated with threaded discussions that guarantees that if you post a question, you will receive a response within 48 hours. That response could be the answer to your question (the preferred result), or it could be that the community is working on it and they'll get back to you later with the answer. Or in some cases, it might be that the community doesn't think it can answer that question. But at least you'll receive an answer within a specified time

and you'll know whether you need to seek a different avenue.

Finally, some communities need to be allowed to die. If a community has failed to build its membership, no longer has active members, or no longer has a viable purpose, the right thing to do is to retire it. Move on to another topic of greater relevance and currency which can attract new members who are passionate about it.

Require community participation

As part of the individual KM goals defined for employees, one which you may wish to include is to require everyone to belong to at least one community. A very simple way for a KM programme to succeed is if every employee joins and is active in at least one community.

For example, one of the performance goals for all employees is to be an active member of at least one community of practice. To get started, visit the community directory website to find the community or communities that match your job. If you have a particular specialty, join the community for that specialty. If you have both a specialty and a role, for example, a storage sales rep, you may wish to join both the storage community and the sales rep community. If you have multiple roles, then join multiple communities. If you have other topics of interest, join those communities as well.

When you subscribe to the community's threaded discussion, you'll be in touch with other people in the same specialty so you can start finding out more about things that are of interest to you and the role that you play. You'll also have a place where you can ask questions, share your insights, and collaborate with your peers.

Being an active community member means not just subscribing to the threaded discussion, which is easy to do, but also regularly thinking about things that you've learnt which you think others could benefit from knowing, and then taking a moment to post to that community and share that insight. That could take just a few minutes because it's as easy as creating a simple e-mail message, writing a few comments, and hitting send. By doing that, your peers will benefit from what you have shared. Your comments will be entered into the archives, so others who come later to the community can read and benefit from them. By collaborating with your colleagues, you will learn more about your specialty, be able to resolve problems, and earn respect for your expertise.

Include a link to the community directory and to additional documentation. Then send the message to the target audience and post it to the KM programme's website.

Learn more about communities

For more information on communities, see:

- 'Communities of practice: a brief introduction' by Etienne Wenger at http://www.ewenger.com/theory/
- 'Communities for knowledge management' by Steve Denning at http://www.stevedenning.com/ communities_knowledge_ management.html
- '10 Critical Success Factors in Building Communities of Practice'by Richard McDermott at http://www. knowledgeboard.com/lib/3465
- 'A bibliography on communities of practice' by CPsquare and com-prac at http://cofpractice-biblio.wikispaces.com/
- *Books for Community Building* by Michael Burns at http://www.amazon. com/gp/richpub/listmania/fullview/ 2CBSJVLYZCG9F/

- 'Communities of Practice Resources' by Fred Nickols at http://home.att. net/~discon/KM/CoPs.htm

For more in-depth understanding, read one or more of these books:

- *Communities of Practice: The Organizational Frontier* by Etienne Wenger and William M. Snyder http://www. amazon.com/gp/product/B00005RZ9V/
- *Communities of Practice: Learning, Meaning, and Identity* by Etienne Wenger http://www.amazon.com/gp/ product/0521663636/
- *Cultivating Communities of Practice* by Etienne Wenger, Richard McDermott, and William M. Snyder http://www. amazon.com/gp/product/1578513308/
- *CompanyCommand: Unleashing the Power of the Army Profession* by Nancy M. Dixon, Nate Allen, Tony Burgess, Pete Kilner and Steve Schweitzer http://www. amazon.com/gp/product/0976454106/
- *The Social Life of Information* by John Seely Brown and Paul Duguid http://www.amazon.com/gp/ product/1578517087/
- *Knowledge Networks: Innovation Through Communities of Practice* by Paul Hildreth and Chris Kimble http://www. amazon.com/gp/product/159140200X/
- *Going Virtual: Distributed Communities of Practice* by Paul Hildreth http://www. amazon.com/gp/product/159140164X/
- *Leveraging Communities of Practice for Strategic Advantage* by Hubert Saint-Onge and Debra Wallace http://www. amazon.com/gp/product/075067458X/
- *Beyond Communities of Practice: Language Power and Social Context* by David Barton and Karin Tusting http://www.amazon.com/gp/ product/0521544920/

- *Online Communities: Designing Usability and Supporting Sociability* by Jenny Preece http://www.amazon.com/gp/product/0471805998/
- *Building Virtual Communities: Learning and Change in Cyberspace* by K. Ann Renninger and Wesley Shumar http://www.amazon.com/gp/product/0521785588/
- *Designing for Virtual Communities in the Service of Learning* by Sasha Barab, Rob Kling, and James Gray http://www.amazon.com/gp/product/0521520819/
- *The Virtual Community: Homesteading on the Electronic Frontier* by Howard Rheingold http://www.amazon.com/gp/product/0262681218/
- *Communities in Cyberspace* by Marc A. Smith http://www.amazon.com/gp/product/0415191408/
- *Building Learning Communities in Cyberspace: Effective Strategies for the Online Classroom* by Rena Palloff and Keith Pratt http://www.amazon.com/gp/product/0787944602/
- *Collaborating Online: Learning Together in Community* by Rena Palloff and Keith Pratt http://www.amazon.com/gp/product/0787976148/
- *Communities of Practice: Lessons from Leading Collaborative Enterprises* by Simon Lelic http://www.ark-group.com/home/xq/asp/pubid.05FE2EAB-FF4F-457D-AFE6-218DE78F25D4/pTitle.Communities_of_Practice/qx/Publications/Publication.htm

Summary

Most KM programmes include communities as a fundamental component. Some programmes are built entirely around them; one excellent example is Caterpillar – see 'Caterpillar Communities of Practice: Knowledge is Power' by Sue Todd at http://www.corpu.com/newsletter06/cat.asp. Because communities connect people to each other and enable knowledge to flow between them, they are a powerful enabler of knowledge sharing.

Chapter 11: Knowledge Management Maxims

The preceding chapters have identified steps to take and components to use. Here are the main principles you can apply in the course of leading and participating in a KM programme.

KM priorities

- We can use more specific terms than KM when we communicate. Try using learning, sharing, reusing, collaborating, and innovating.
- Place more emphasis on connecting people than on collecting documents. People can provide documents at the time of need if you provide an easy way for them to collaborate.
- We aim to learn from mistakes, but keep repeating them. Reduce the stigma of discussing failures, provide ways to do so, and reward those who do.

Innovation

- The sooner you try an idea, the better. When a good suggestion is made, figure out a way to quickly test it.
- A pilot project can be useful immediately. You can learn how to improve the concept from the users.
- Copious planning is not as good as rapid prototyping and frequent incremental improvement. Develop a complete but simple plan, review it with key people, revise it based on their suggestions, implement it, assess progress, and adjust as necessary.

Communities

- Be as inclusive as possible. The more diverse the backgrounds and opinions in a community, the more learning and innovation can result.
- Take some time to stimulate community conversations. Don't wait for an issue to be raised by someone else. Prime the pump as needed to keep the discussion going.
- Face-to-face knowledge sharing is not a luxury. It is essential to building and sustaining trust. Plan for periodic meetings where the community can make and renew personal bonds.

Killer application for social networking

- Find a killer application for social networking within your company. A killer application is one that large numbers of voluntary users tell their friends about.
- A killer application will encourage people to sign up and maintain their personal information and networks. This will provide better information than mandatory expertise locators.
- Link key knowledge initiatives to this killer application. This will help to increase awareness of other applications which might otherwise be ignored.

Leadership

- Leaders should be open, honest, accessible and responsive. People follow leaders who are straightforward, inspirational and fair.

Leadership

- Set no more than three goals. Keep them simple and easy to remember.
- Leaders must command respect through words and deeds. They should model the behaviours they wish their followers to adopt.

Communications

- Good communication matters. Use language carefully, correctly and clearly.
- Avoid buzzwords and jargon. If you don't, your audience will ignore your messages.
- Tell the truth. People can easily tell when you are lying. If you lie, you will never be able to regain trust.

Participation

- Most people are reluctant to speak up. They prefer others to lead discussions. Providing good leaders allows others to learn while lurking.
- People are more willing to enter questions electronically on a conference call than to speak up and ask a question on the phone. Offer this option and assign someone to read the questions received this way.
- People are more willing to talk about a success than they are to write about it. Find ways to get them to talk about their successes. You can assign someone to transcribe the conversation and enter it into a document, thus transforming tacit knowledge into explicit knowledge.

Crowd behaviour

- People jump on bandwagons, follow fads, and thoughtlessly use the latest buzzwords. Try to get them to adopt elements of the KM programme as the latest trend, but then deliver benefits that keep them on board.
- Widely send out a request for input and you will receive a limited number of replies. Target such requests to those who are likely to reply.
- Send an e-mail to a large distribution list and it may be perceived as spam. Keep push communications to a minimum. Instead, offer opt-in subscriptions.

Personal growth

- Don't hide – engage. Take a risk, get outside your comfort zone and challenge yourself to try something new. You will grow and develop.
- Submit an abstract for a presentation at a conference. Write a paper and send it to a publication. Start a blog. You will be rewarded by the results.
- Try out tools and processes yourself. Learn first-hand what works and what doesn't. You will be able to empathise with other users, learn useful techniques and become recognised as an expert. Be hands-on, use the tools of the trade and practice what you preach.

Networking

- Expand your personal network. Talk to other attendees at conferences. Post to threaded discussions. Contact other people, including those who don't know you and those who are famous. You will be surprised at how many people will be glad to interact with you, become part of your network, and join a community you lead or participate in.
- Share relentlessly. Look at each piece of information you receive, read or

create and ask "who else could use this?" Then send it to them. They will appreciate your consideration.

- When you contact someone else, even if just to share a minor piece of information, it will often lead to an unexpected benefit. They will be prompted to ask you a question, share an idea, or make a suggestion that will be helpful.
- Rely on your colleagues. Ask them to review what you are working on and they will give you good advice. If you do good things for others without concern for what's in it for you, your colleagues will be glad to reciprocate.

Critical success factors

- Get the senior executive to play an active role. The senior executive should be a champion who endlessly promotes the initiative. Leaders who participate with a high level of personal energy will convey the importance of the programme.
- Promote only those who share their knowledge. Establish knowledge sharing as a requirement for career advancement. When people are promoted, communicate the details of the knowledge they have shared.
- Recognise and reward desired behaviours. Use frequent contributor programmes, incentive points systems, and publications featuring selected submissions.
- Dedicate resources. Assign a dedicated team for project leadership, development, administration, and support. This focused team provides the effort needed for the programme to succeed.

Conclusion
Pundits are usually wrong. Consider all expert advice with some skepticism. Develop your own maxims based on your experience.

Additional insights
Many authors have written about other KM principles: here are some examples.

In 'Developing a Knowledge-Based Theory of the Firm' by Claus Otto Scharmer at http://www.dialogonleadership.org/vonKrogh-1999.html Georg von Krogh discusses three topics:

Stages of KM

- Capturing knowledge.
- Sharing and transferring knowledge.
- Generating new knowledge.

Blind spots

- Sources of rent.
- High mobility and low loyalty of human capital.
- The task-creating company.
- The role of leadership in the knowledge economy.

Importance of care

- Care is a gift.
- Care drives attention.

In 'Complex Acts of Knowing – Paradox and Descriptive Self Awareness' at http://www.cognitive-edge.com/articledetails.php?articleid=13 Dave Snowden describes three generations of KM:

1. First generation focused on timely information provision for decision

support and in support of business process reengineeering initiatives.

2. Second generation focused on tacit-explicit knowledge conversion.
3. Third generation requires the clear separation of context, narrative and content management.

   a) Complex adaptive systems theory is used to create a sense-making model that identifies a natural flow model of knowledge creation, disruption, and utilisation.
   b) Knowledge is seen paradoxically as both a thing and a flow requiring diverse management approaches.

In 'Volunteer not conscript' at http://www.cognitive-edge.com/2006/08/volunteer_not_conscript.php Snowden lists three rules of KM:

1. Knowledge will only ever be volunteered; it cannot be conscripted.
2. We only know what we know when we need to know it.
3. We always know more than we can tell and we will always tell more than we can write down.
4. And a new formulation of the first rule:

   If you ask someone, or a body for specific knowledge in the context of a real need it will never be refused. If you ask them to give you your knowledge on the basis that you may need it in the future, then you will never receive it.

In 'Our take on how to talk about knowledge management' at http://www.anecdote.com.au/papers/AnecdoteOurTakeOnKM.pdf Mark Schenk, Shawn Callahan and Andrew Rixon list these characteristics of knowledge:

- You cannot command people's knowledge; you need to encourage them to share it.
- We always know more than we can tell, and we can always tell more that we can write.
- We only know what we know when we need to know it.
- If knowledge is to be converted to information and *vice versa*, people must do virtually all the work.
- Knowledge is sticky; it does not flow easily across organisation boundaries.
- Trust is an essential prerequisite for effective knowledge sharing in organisations.
- When solving problems, our natural tendency is to ask questions.
- Efficiency encourages codification; effectiveness encourages lower levels of codification and greater flexibility.
- Sharing is a natural act.

In *The Wealth of Knowledge: Intellectual Capital and the Twenty-first Century Organization* (http://www.amazon.com/gp/product/0385500726/) on pages 314–315, under 'Measuring the Efficiency of Knowledge Work and Knowledge Workers' Thomas Stewart provides a list from Wouter deVries of a dozen factors critical to the success of a KM project or initiative:

- Knowledge vision: do we know what knowledge we need for this project or in this line of business?
- A clear connection to performance: will this save money? Grow sales? And so on.
- A knowledge-friendly structure: e.g., teams *versus* functional silos.
- A knowledge-friendly culture: do people share or hoard?
- Adequacy of resources.

- Technical infrastructure: how good are our KM tools?
- Knowledge structure: have we established a vocabulary and taxonomy for the knowledge we are using?
- Motivation: are the right incentives in place?
- Clarity of purpose and goals.
- Is there a common terminology about KM itself?
- Top management support.
- Power: how great is our ability to break through any organisational barriers we encounter?

In 'The Eleven Deadliest Sins Of Knowledge Management' (California Management Review Vol. 40, No. 3, 1998, pages 265–275) Liam Fahey and Laurence Prusak list 11 errors made in the practice of KM:

- Not developing a working definition of knowledge.
- Emphasising knowledge stock to the detriment of knowledge flow.
- Viewing knowledge as existing predominantly outside of the heads of individuals.
- Not understanding that a fundamental intermediate purpose of managing knowledge is to create shared context.
- Paying little heed to the role and importance of tacit knowledge.
- Disentangling knowledge from its uses.
- Downplaying thinking and reasoning.
- Focusing on the past and the present and not the future.
- Failing to recognise the importance of experimentation.
- Substituting technological contact for human interface.
- Seeking to develop direct measures of knowledge.

Kaye Vivian revisited this list in 'The 11 Deadliest Sins of KM (revisited)' at http://dove-lane.com/index.php/?p=117:

- Failing to define knowledge.
- Emphasising content artifacts instead of knowledge flow.
- Believing knowledge can exist outside the heads of individuals.
- Believing that creating shared context is not an important milestone in the process of managing knowledge.
- Failing to understand the role and significance of tacit knowledge.
- Confusing information creation with applying knowledge to new situations.
- Overlooking the importance of thinking and reasoning to the KM process.
- Documenting the past and present, and ignoring the future.
- Failing to acknowledge the importance of experimentation and failure.
- Substituting technological contact for face-to-face interactions.
- Attempting to measure knowledge using the metrics of balance sheets.

Vivian then reformulated the list into 'The 11 Axioms of Knowledge Management' at http://dove-lane.com/index.php/?p=121.

Knowledge can be defined

- Corollary: We have not yet defined knowledge.
- Corollary: We have not yet defined knowledge management.

Knowledge management is a process dependent upon people and what they know

- Corollary: Knowledge management generates information artifacts.

- Corollary: Information artifacts are used to generate new knowledge.
- Corollary: Knowledge cannot be codified.

Knowledge cannot exist outside the heads of individuals

- Corollary: Information can.

Knowledge exchange requires a shared context between individuals

- Corollary: Knowledge can be exchanged or created within a shared context.

Tacit knowledge is the true knowledge and cannot be managed

- Corollary: To capture tacit knowledge is to make it explicit and convert it to information.

Applications of knowledge are not the same as knowledge

- Corollary: Using knowledge is not knowledge management.
- Corollary: Knowledge is separate from its uses.

Thinking and reasoning are the engine of the KM process

- Corollary: Thinking and reasoning result in knowledge.
- Corollary: Communicating the results of thinking and reasoning creates information artifacts.

Documenting the past has value when no changes are anticipated

- Corollary: The future can be influenced by today's thinking and reasoning.

- Corollary: Documenting the past is content management.

Experimentation is crucial to improvement

- Corollary: Experimentation will occasionally result in failure.
- Corollary: Experimentation can result in big successes.

Human interactions cannot be replaced by technology

- Corollary: Knowledge development and exchange occurs in people's brains.
- Corollary: Technology provides a means to capture discussions and convert them to information artifacts.
- Corollary: Knowledge management is not technology.

Knowledge cannot be measured directly

- Corollary: Knowledge has value to an organisation.
- Corollary: Conventional balance sheet metrics do not adequately measure knowledge.
- Corollary: Information resulting from knowledge management can be measured.

In '12 Principles of Knowledge Management' at http://www.providersedge. com/docs/km_articles/12_Principles_of_ Knowledge_Management.pdf Verna Allee explains:

1. Knowledge is messy. Because knowledge is connected to everything else, you can't isolate the knowledge aspect of anything neatly. In the knowledge universe, you can't pay attention to just one factor.

2. Knowledge is self-organising. The self that knowledge organises around is organisational or group identity and purpose.

3. Knowledge seeks community. Knowledge wants to happen, just as life wants to happen. Both want to happen as community. Nothing illustrates this principle more than the Internet.

4. Knowledge travels via language. Without a language to describe our experience, we can't communicate what we know. Expanding organisational knowledge means that we must develop the languages we use to describe our work experience.

5. The more you try to pin knowledge down, the more it slips away. It's tempting to try to tie up knowledge as codified knowledge-documents, patents, libraries, databases, and so forth. But too much rigidity and formality regarding knowledge lead to the stultification of creativity.

6. Looser is probably better. Highly adaptable systems look sloppy. The survival rate of diverse, decentralised systems is higher. That means we can waste resources and energy trying to control knowledge too tightly.

7. There is no one solution. Knowledge is always changing. For the moment, the best approach to managing it is one that keeps things moving along while keeping options open.

8. Knowledge doesn't grow forever. Eventually, some knowledge is lost or dies, just as things in nature. Unlearning and letting go of old ways of thinking, even retiring whole blocks of knowledge, contribute to the vitality and evolution of knowledge.

9. No one is in charge. Knowledge is a social process. That means no one person can take responsibility for collective knowledge.

10. You can't impose rules and systems. If knowledge is truly self-organising, the most important way to advance it is to remove the barriers to self-organisation. In a supportive environment, knowledge will take care of itself.

11. There is no silver bullet. There is no single leverage point or best practice to advance knowledge. It must be supported at multiple levels and in a variety of ways.

12. How you define knowledge determines how you manage it. The 'knowledge question' can present itself many ways. For example, concern about the ownership of knowledge leads to acquiring codified knowledge that is protected by copyrights and patents.

In 'The seven basics of knowledge management' at http://www.stevedenning.com/seven_basics_knowledge_management.html Steve Denning lists:

- Strategy
- Organisation
- Budget
- Incentives
- Community
- Technology
- Measurement

In 'Six laws of knowledge management' at http://www.stevedenning.com/laws_knowledge_management.html Denning says:

- Knowledge is key to business survival.
- Communities are the heart and soul of knowledge sharing.
- Virtual communities need physical interaction.
- Passion drives communities of practice.

- Knowledge sharing has an inside-out and an outside-in dimension.
- Storytelling ignites knowledge sharing.

In '13 Myths of Knowledge Management' at http://www.stevedenning.com/slides/SIKM-MythsOfKM.pdf Denning lists:

The nature of knowledge

- Knowledge is always a plus.
- Knowledge is sticky.
- The concept of knowledge is infinitely extendable.

The nature of knowledge sharing

- Knowledge can be transferred.
- Knowledge-sharing is always a good thing.
- Knowledge is more important than values.
- People always want to have better knowledge.
- The task of KM is to enhance the supply of knowledge.
- There are structural solutions to the lack of demand for knowledge.

The impact of knowledge sharing

- Knowledge management will transform the business landscape.
- KM succeeded and no one knows it.
- It was the IT vendors who killed KM.
- Knowledge is the only sustainable competitive advantage.

In '10 steps to get more business value from knowledge management' at http://www.stevedenning.com/slides/GettingValueFromKM-Final-Aug06.pdf Denning says:

1. Slice through the hype.
2. Fight off the IT firms.

3. Take a hard look at your own organisation.
4. Set your KM strategy.
5. Use narrative techniques to communicate your KM strategy.
6. Pay special attention to organisational values.
7. Encourage communities and cross-communities.
8. Set your incentives (carefully!).
9. Measure progress (carefully!).
10. Recognise the limits of knowledge.

In 'Knowledge Flows: Mainstream or Myths?' at http://dev.skyrme.com/updates/u73_f2.htm David Skyrme offers ten points of conventional wisdom which may or may not be true:

1. Knowledge can't be managed.
2. Best practices aren't best practices.
3. Communities don't practice.
4. Storytelling isn't just telling stories.
5. Expertise directories locate your experts.
6. A portal is a gateway to knowledge.
7. What you can measure you can manage.
8. The biggest obstacle to knowledge sharing is corporate culture.
9. E-learning and KM are two sides of the same coin.
10. Increasing creativity will increase innovation.

In 'KM principles' at http://denham.typepad.com/km/2006/08/km_principles.html Denham Grey advises the following:

- Choose engagement over a repository.
- Respect and appreciate the key role of trust and context.
- Collect stories, use metaphor, ethnography and analogy to build inquiry.

- Cultivate executive support.
- The essence of KM:
  - increasing awareness;
  - fostering learning;
  - supporting sense making.

In '5 most important KM issues' at http://denham.typepad.com/km/2005/11/5_most_importan.html Grey provides two lists:

Five most critical issues facing Knowledge Leaders today

1. Cultivating awareness of the knowledge imperative and advantage in our connected, global economy.
2. Connecting (local) knowledge actions with the (overall) business direction.
3. Building a culture that encourages the creation of new knowledge and making sharing happen.
4. Moving conversations into virtual space to surface assumptions, extend reach, improve brainstorming and leverage many to many communication.
5. Selecting a suitable, stable, scaleable technology to support a people centric knowledge strategy.

Five most critical issues facing Knowledge Leaders over the next three to five years

1. Taking a successful KM strategy to all stakeholders (suppliers, customers and investors).
2. Making knowledge work invisible – i.e., so well integrated it becomes a part of who we are and what we do!
3. Building relationships so knowledge can flow, but keeping key inventions tacit to prevent leakage.
4. Crafting ontologies (taxonomies) so firms can use the emergent technology of meta-inference and

apply advanced search and intelligent agents.
5. Keeping the focus on core KM issues (learning, collaboration, relationships, dialogue, critical thinking) when the next management fad (complexity?) arrives.

In 'Six Eyes of Seeing Knowledge' at http://knowledgefutures.wordpress.com/2006/08/29/six-eyes-of-seeing-knowledge/ Luke Naismith explores "the hidden assumption that intellectual knowledge is the only lens for creating and sharing knowledge. Other eyes for seeing and sense making have the potential to uncover new knowledge:"

1. Intellect – arguably the most important eye. The basis of our logic, rationality and learning. Uses science as the metanarrative. Leads to information and intelligence (and knowledge of course).
2. Instinct – knowledge gained from our initial response to sensory input without cognitive thinking processes. Able to form quick conclusions in a 'blink' (Malcolm Gladwell). Knowledge here leads to immediacy of response but can lead to incorrect generalisations and stereotyping.
3. Imagination – knowledge gained from our dreams, aspirations and visions. From this knowledge we gain intention and inspiration.
4. Intuition – knowledge gained from emotional rather than intellectual understanding based on our relationships with others. From this knowledge we gain integrity and interconnectivity. It includes the notion of morphic resonance (Sheldrake), microvita (Sarkar) and emotional intelligence (Goleman).

5. Insight – knowledge gained from our creative processes using theta waves. Happens best in the shower (or in Archimedes' case, the bath). Happens when we are not thinking about things. Knowledge here gives us improvisation happening in-time.

6. Ignorance – this is our hidden knowledge – what we don't see. By focusing only on what we know, we miss the areas that we don't know. KM is as much about managing our ignorance as it is about managing our knowledge. From our ignorance, we gain inquiry leading to interventions.

The new middle class, Thomas Friedman says (http://www.panasianbiz.com/2006/04/thomas_friedman_columnist_new.html), will be made up of workers in eight fields:

1. Collaborators – people who can tie things together, even people of different cultures.
2. Leveragers – people who know how to leverage technology to meet needs.
3. Synthesisers – people who can connect the dots.
4. Localisers – people who can use technology to start businesses from their garages; bring global resources to their neighbourhood.
5. Passionate personalisers – people who can make people excited about simple/everyday things/anything.
6. Anything green – people who do good for the environment.
7. Explainers – people who can explain and make sense of it all, teachers, online media.
8. Adapters – the people who train for the Olympics but don't know what event they will participate – the people who are really flexible in many fields.

In 'The Innovation Sandbox' at http://www.strategy-business.com/press/freearticle/06306 C.K. Prahalad writes that companies in any industry, in any country, can adopt a sandbox approach to breakthrough innovation. But it requires accepting a few premises that are counterintuitive to many managers:

- Radically rethink the entire business model: technology choices, scale, workflow, and organisation.
- In addition to researching the field, get immersed in the lives of the target users. There are tough challenges in access, awareness, affordability, and availability, and only those who are grounded in the reality of their users' work will understand their priorities. The users themselves may not articulate their needs.
- Accept constraints. You cannot do all things; you must do a few things very well. Many people have come to believe that creativity must be unconstrained; in practice, however, breakthrough creativity requires an explicit acknowledgment of limits.
- Don't innovate in isolation. Breakthroughs occur when there are clusters of innovations, taking place continuously over time, in small experiments from which companies learn rapidly, and in an ecosystem involving many collaborators and partners.
- None of these changes will be possible without a clear and unflagging commitment to a strategic intent.

In 'Sense-Making' at http://www.kwork.org/Stars/kennedy.html Mary Lee Kennedy quotes Karl Weick from his book *Making Sense of the Organization* at http://www.amazon.com/gp/product/0631223193/ to define seven properties of sense making:

1. Social context, i.e., the actual, implied or imagined presence of others.
2. Personal identity, i.e., a person's sense of who he or she is in a given setting: what threats to this sense of self the setting contains: and what is available to enhance it.
3. Retrospect, i.e., the perceived world is actually a past world in the sense that things are visualised and seen before they are conceptualised.
4. Salient clues, i.e., the resourcefulness with which people elaborate tiny indicators into full-blown stories, typically a self-fulfilling prophecy or application of the documentary method (he sees this as key to what sense making is all about).
5. Ongoing projects, i.e., sense making is constrained by the speed with which events flow into the past and events become outdated.
6. Plausibility, i.e., coherence, how events hang together.
7. Enactment, i.e., action to gain some sense of what one is up against by asking questions, making declarations, through prototypes, through probes to see how something reacts.

In 'Sensemaking, Knowledge Creation, and Decision Making: Organizational Knowing as Emergent Strategy' at http://choo.fis. utoronto.ca/OUP/Chap5/default.html Chun Wei Choo lists:

Three kinds of knowledge

1. Tacit knowledge in the expertise and experience of individuals.
2. Explicit or rule-based knowledge in artifacts, rules and routines.
3. Cultural knowledge in the assumptions and beliefs used by members to assign value and significance to new information or knowledge.

Three kinds of knowledge creation

1. Knowledge conversion: the organisation continuously creates new knowledge by converting between the personal, tacit knowledge of individuals who develop creative insight, and the shared, explicit knowledge by which the organisation develops new products and innovations.
2. Knowledge integration: the result of the organisation's ability to coordinate and integrate the knowledge of many individual specialists.
3. Knowledge transfer: across organisational boundaries; can involve tacit, explicit, and cultural knowledge to varying degrees.

Four modes of organisational decision-making

1. Boundedly rational mode: goal and procedural clarity are both high, choice is guided by performance programmes.
2. Process mode: goals are clear but the methods to attain them are not; decision-making becomes a process divided into three phases:

   - Identification: recognises the need for decision and develops an understanding of the decision issues;
   - Development: activates search and design routines to develop one or more solutions to address a problem, crisis, or opportunity;
   - Selection: evaluates the alternatives and chooses a solution for commitment to action.

3. Political mode: contested by interest groups, but procedural certainty is high within the groups; each group believes

that its preferred alternative is best for the organisation.

4. Anarchic mode: goal and procedural uncertainty are both high; decision situations consist of relatively independent streams of problems, solutions, participants, and choice opportunities arriving and leaving; a decision then happens when problems, solutions, participants, and choices coincide.

In 'Sharing Knowledge by Design: Building Intellectual Capital in a Virtual World' at http://www.chrysalisinternational.com/uploads/communique_020106.htm Nancy Settle-Murphy writes: "One relatively modest knowledge-sharing system may be the springboard by which an enterprise-wide system is born" and offers ten suggestions:

- Sell the benefits.
- Appoint a KM leader who can dedicate meaningful time to building the right infrastructure.
- Set up a community of practice (CoP) to start.
- Create a formal repository in which knowledge can be dropped off.
- Think globally.
- Encourage the sharing of knowledge by embedding related activities within existing work processes.
- Reward those who show special initiative in sharing knowledge.
- Cultivate senior management as champions.
- Create a network of knowledge advisors.
- Open the lines of communications among KM subject matter experts, regardless of their exact titles, roles and locations.

In 'The Knowledge Management Domain: Knowledge Management Approach to

Knowledge Management' at http://www.kminstitute.org/The_KM_Domain_October_2003.pdf Steven Wieneke and Karla Phlypo-Price use KM techniques to define the domain of KM. Their paper asserts that the Knowledge Management Domain is made up of at least eight disciplines comprising 50 specialties or dimensions.

Each specialty or dimension has two thresholds, one for initiation and another for sustainability. Between and on either side of the thresholds is a spectrum of metrics which measure the maturity of each specialty/dimension. The Domain and the spectra can be used to appraise the initiation readiness or the sustainability of a knowledge-based, learning organisation. Additionally, the Domain and spectra can be used to create tactical and strategic KM initiatives. Wieneke and Phlypo-Price define up to seven core competencies for each specialty or dimension.

The disciplines are:

1. Knowledge arenas.
2. Knowledge capital.
3. Knowledge-based learning process.
4. Enterprise-wide infrastructure.
5. Knowledge arena benchmarking.
6. Knowledge arena content management.
7. Learning organisation.
8. Enterprise-wide knowledge socialisation.

In 'European Guide to good Practice in Knowledge Management – Part 1: Knowledge Management Framework' at ftp://cenftp1.cenorm.be/PUBLIC/CWAs/e-Europe/KM/CWA14924-01-2004-Mar.pdf CEN, the European Committee for Standardization, provides the following framework:

1. What, why and how to use?
2. Core value-adding processes.

3. Core knowledge activities.
4. Enablers for KM.

   a) Personal knowledge capabilities.
      ○ Ambition.
      ○ Skills.
      ○ Behaviour.
      ○ Methods, tools and techniques.
      ○ Time management.
      ○ Personal knowledge.

   b) Organisational knowledge capabilities.
      ○ Mission, vision and strategy.
      ○ Culture.
      ○ Process and Organisation.
      ○ Measurement.
      ○ Technology and infrastructure.
      ○ Knowledge assets.

5. KM implementation and change management.

In 'Common Attributes of Knowledge Work and Knowledge Workers' at http://www.babsonknowledge. org/2005/10/6_common_attributes_ of_knowled.htm Tom Davenport observes six basic principles:

1. Knowledge workers like autonomy.
2. Specifying the detailed steps and flow of knowledge-intensive processes is less valuable and more difficult than for other types of work.
3. "You can observe a lot by watching."
4. Knowledge workers usually have good reasons for doing what they do.
5. Commitment matters.
6. Knowledge workers value their knowledge, and don't share it easily.

Professor Paul Dorsey and colleagues at Millikin University defined seven Personal

Knowledge Management (PKM) skills (http:// www.millikin.edu/pkm/pkm_ascue.html):

1. Retrieving information.
2. Evaluating information.
3. Organising information.
4. Collaborating around information.
5. Analysing information.
6. Presenting information.
7. Securing information.

In Tom Davenport's *Thinking for a Living* (http://www.amazon.com/gp/ product/1591394236/), he addresses many topics related to PKM. In Chapter 6 ('Developing Individual Knowledge Worker Capabilities'), he lists ten common attributes of individuals who are highly effective in managing their own personal information environments:

1. They avoided gadgets.
2. Limited the number of separate devices.
3. Invested effort in organising information.
4. Weren't missionaries.
5. Got help.
6. Used assistants – to some degree.
7. Weren't doctrinaire about paper *versus* electronic approaches.
8. Decided what information was important to them, and organised it particularly well.
9. Use lists.
10. Adapt the use of tools and approaches to the work situation at a given time.

For more information on personal knowledge management, see:

■ 'Your say: Personal knowledge management' by Sandra Higgison at http://www.ikmagazine.com/xq/asp/ articleid.DDDD6EE3-47C6-49CD- 9070-F1B1547FD29F/eTitle.Your_say_

Personal_knowledge_management/
qx/display.htm

- 'Personal KM Q&A' by Lilia Efimova
  at http://blog.mathemagenic.com/
  stories/2004/09/07/personalKmQa.html
- 'Connecting Personal KM to
  Innovation' by Thomas Collins at
  http://knowledgeaforethought.blogs.
  com/knowledge_aforethought/2004/02/
  connecting_pers.html
- 'Personal Knowledge Management'
  by Dave Pollard at http://blogs.
  salon.com/0002007/2004/02/26.
  html#a642 and http://blogs.salon.
  com/0002007/2005/11/23.
  html#a1349
- 'Personal toolkit: A framework for
  personal knowledge management
  tools' by Steve Barth at http://www.
  kmworld.com/Articles/ReadArticle.
  aspx?ArticleID=9416
- Gurteen Topic at http://www.gurteen.
  com/gurteen/gurteen.nsf/id/pkm

Summary

Out of these and other lists of maxims, guidelines, and definitions, choose the ones which sound the best to you. Add your own based on your personal experience. Apply them whenever a relevant question, challenge, or opportunity arises.

I hope that this report has helped you *learn* more about how to start and run a knowledge management initiative. You may wish to *share* what you have learnt with others in your organisation. I encourage you to *reuse* the ideas and examples in your own programme and *collaborate* with colleagues from other programmes. From this starting point, you will likely be able to *innovate* based on your own circumstances, ideas, and experience. This is truly an example of practicing what you preach.

Appendix: Resources for learning about the field

Books

Here are 25 books recommended to get you started.

1. *The Knowledge Evolution: Expanding Organizational Intelligence* by Verna Allee http://www.amazon.com/gp/product/075069842X/

2. *The Future of Knowledge: Increasing Prosperity through Value Networks* by Verna Allee http://www.amazon.com/gp/product/0750675918/

3. *Next Generation Knowledge Management* by Jerry Ash, featuring key contributions from: Stephen Denning, Leif Edvinsson, Karl-Erik Sveiby, David Snowden, Hubert Saint-Onge, Carl Frappaolo, Debra Amidon, Ash Sooknanan, Richard Cross, and Carol Kinsey Goman http://www.ark-group.com/home/xq/asp/pubid.DEE5993B-3AA5-4F32-9BF9-DC2912FBC2B4/pTitle.Next_Generation_Knowledge_Management/qx/Publications/Publication.htm

4. *The Strategic Management of Intellectual Capital and Organizational Knowledge* by Chun Wei Choo and Nick Bontis http://www.amazon.com/gp/product/019513866X/

5. *The Social Life of Information* by John Seely Brown and Paul Duguid http://www.amazon.com/gp/product/1578517087/

6. *The Knowing Organization: How Organizations Use Information To Construct Meaning, Create Knowledge, and Make Decisions* by Chun Wei Choo http://www.amazon.com/gp/product/0195110129/

7. *Learning to Fly: Practical Knowledge Management from Leading and Learning Organizations* by Chris Collison and Geoff Parcell http://www.amazon.com/gp/product/1841125091/

8. *Working Knowledge* by Thomas Davenport and Laurence Prusak http://www.amazon.com/gp/product/1578513014/

9. *Thinking for a Living: How to Get Better Performances And Results from Knowledge Workers* by Thomas Davenport http://www.amazon.com/gp/product/1591394236/

10. *The Leader's Guide to Storytelling: Mastering the Art and Discipline of Business Narrative* by Stephen Denning http://www.amazon.com/gp/product/078797675X/

11. *Common Knowledge: How Companies Thrive by Sharing What They Know* by Nancy M. Dixon http://www.amazon.com/gp/product/0875849040/

12. *CompanyCommand: Unleashing the Power of the Army Profession* by Nancy M. Dixon, Nate Allen, Tony Burgess, Pete Kilner and Steve Schweitzer http://www.amazon.com/gp/product/0976454106/

13. *Intellectual Capital: Realizing Your Company's True Value by Finding Its Hidden Brainpower* by Leif Edvinsson and Michael Malone http://www.amazon.com/gp/product/0887308414/

14. *Deep Smarts: How to Cultivate and Transfer Enduring Business Wisdom* by Dorothy Leonard and Walter

Swap http://www.amazon.com/gp/
product/1591395283/

15. *If Only We Knew What We Know: The
Transfer of Internal Knowledge and
Best Practice* by Carla O'Dell and C.
Jackson Grayson http://www.amazon.
com/gp/product/0684844745/

16. *The Knowing-Doing Gap: How Smart
Companies Turn Knowledge into
Action* by Jeffrey Pfeffer and Robert
Sutton http://www.amazon.com/gp/
product/1578511240/

17. *Complete Idiot's Guide to Knowledge
Management* by Melissie Rumizen
http://www.amazon.com/gp/
product/0028641779/

18. *Leveraging Communities of Practice for
Strategic Advantage* by Hubert Saint-
Onge, Debra Wallace http://www.
amazon.com/gp/product/075067458X/

19. *Knowing Knowledge* by George Siemens
http://www.knowingknowledge.com/
book.php

20. *Intellectual Capital: The New Wealth
of Organizations* by Thomas A.
Stewart http://www.amazon.com/gp/
product/0385483813/

21. *The Wealth of Knowledge: Intellectual
Capital and the Twenty-first Century
Organization* by Thomas A. Stewart
http://www.amazon.com/gp/
product/0385500726/

22. *The New Organizational Wealth:
Managing & Measuring Knowledge-
Based Assets* by Karl Erik Sveiby
http://www.amazon.com/gp/
product/1576750140/

23. *Enabling Knowledge Creation:
How to Unlock the Mystery of Tacit
Knowledge and Release the Power
of Innovation* by Georg von Krogh,
Kazuo Ichijo, and Ikujiro Nonaka
http://www.amazon.com/gp/
product/0195126165/

24. *Communities of Practice: Learning,
Meaning, and Identity* by Etienne
Wenger http://www.amazon.com/gp/
product/0521663636/

25. *Cultivating Communities of Practice* by
Etienne Wenger, Richard McDermott, &
William M. Snyder http://www.amazon.
com/gp/product/1578513308/

For additional information on books, see:

1. Verna Allee's Recommended Books
http://www.vernaallee.com/VA/
Recommended_Books.html

2. Amazon Listmania by Nick Bontis
http://www.amazon.com/gp/richpub/
listmania/fullview/35VB1WHT82EXZ/

3. Amazon Listmania! by M. Audran
Sevrain http://www.amazon.com/
gp/richpub/listmania/fullview/
31GQW5P03WBMG/

4. Ark Group Reports http://www.ark-
group.com/home/publication.asp#reps

5. Barnes & Noble http://browse.
barnesandnoble.com/browse/nav.asp?z
=y&visgrp=nonfiction&N=913394

6. Elsevier Butterworth-Heinemann
http://books.elsevier.com/
knowledgemanagement/

7. Gurteen Knowledge Website Books
http://www.gurteen.com/gurteen/
gurteen.nsf/id/books

8. *Inside Knowledge* Magazine's
KM University articles
http://www.ikmagazine.com/

9. KnowledgeBoard: The 42 books to
start your Knowledge-Management
own bibliography http://www.
knowledgeboard.com/cgi-bin/item.
cgi?id=1319

10. Line56's KM Blog features a weekly
section on recommended books http://
www.line56.com/blogs/contributor_
index.asp?ContributorID=1

Periodicals

Here are ten periodicals to which you can subscribe.

1. Ark Group Inside Knowledge http://www.ikmagazine.com/currentissue.asp
2. destinationKM http://www.destinationkm.com/
3. Gurteen Knowledge-Letter http://www.gurteen.com/gurteen/gurteen.nsf/(Views)/WebNewsList?OpenDocument&Count=999
4. Journal of Knowledge Management http://www.emeraldinsight.com/info/journals/jkm/jkm.jsp
5. KMWorld http://www.kmworld.com/
6. KnowledgeBoard Newswires http://www.knowledgeboard.com/pastnews/index.html
7. K Street Directions http://www.knowledgestreet.com/About_Us/Directions/directions.html
8. Melcrum KM Review http://www.melcrum.com/cgi-bin/melcrum/eu_content.pl?docurl=topic%20km
9. Montague Institute Review http://www.montague.com/review/review.html
10. Steve Denning's newsletter about organisational storytelling http://www.stevedenning.com/

Websites

The following ten websites are recommended for learning more about KM.

1. AOK http://www.kwork.org/index.html
2. APQC http://www.apqc.org/portal/apqc/site
3. Brint KMNetwork and WWW Virtual Library on Knowledge Management http://km.brint.com/
4. Buckman Laboratories: Knowledge Nurture http://www.knowledge-nurture.com/

5. CIO KM Research Center http://www.cio.com/research/knowledge/
6. Gurteen Knowledge Website http://www.gurteen.com/gurteen/gurteen.nsf/
7. The Kaieteur Institute For Knowledge Management http://www.kikm.org/
8. KmWiki http://kmwiki.wikispaces.com/
9. KnowledgeBoard http://www.knowledgeboard.com/index.html
10. KNOW Network http://www.knowledgebusiness.com/

Subscribe to blogs and news using syndicated feeds

My Yahoo! supports the various flavours of RSS and Atom, allowing you to add virtually anything to your page. This is a good way to monitor news and blogs from a single website. For more information, see http://my.yahoo.com/s/about/new_migrate.html.

Here are details on KM aggregators, periodicals, websites, and blogs which offer RSS feeds. The first link is to the website, and the second is either the URL to use for the RSS feed (RSS – copy and paste this into your reader), or a website containing multiple RSS feeds from which to choose (feeds – visit the site and copy the link you prefer).

Aggregators

1. Blogdigger http://groups.blogdigger.com/groups.jsp?id=2650
   RSS http://groups.blogdigger.com/rss.jsp?id=2650
2. del.icio.us http://del.icio.us/tag/knowledge%2Bmanagement
   RSS http://del.icio.us/rss/tag/knowledge+management
3. Planet KM http://planetkm.org/
   RSS http://planetkm.org/rss20.xml

4. Technorati http://www.technorati.com/ tag/knowledge%20management **RSS** http://feeds.technorati.com/feed/ posts/tag/knowledge%20management
5. topix.net http://www.topix.net/business/ knowledge-management **RSS** http://rss.topix.net/rss/business/ knowledge-management.xml

Periodicals

1. Ark Group *Inside Knowledge* http:// www.ikmagazine.com/e-newsletter.asp **RSS** http://www.ikmagazine.com/ freerss.asp
2. iKMS Newsletter http://knowledge. typepad.com/ikms_newsletter/ **RSS** http://knowledge.typepad.com/ ikms_newsletter/atom.xml
3. KMWorld http://www.kmworld.com/news/ Feeds http://www.kmworld.com/RSS/ **RSS**_Feeds.aspx
4. KnowledgeBoard Newswires http://www.knowledgeboard.com/ pastnews/index.html **RSS** http://www.knowledgeboard.com/ include/xml_rss2_syndicated1.xml
5. Knowledge Flow http://www.library.nhs.uk/ knowledgemanagement/ **RSS** http://www.library.nhs.uk/ knowledgemanagement/RSS/CMS. aspx?feed=14
6. Line56 http://www.line56.com/ Feeds http://www.line56.com/rss/
7. Melcrum KM Review http://www. melcrum.com/cgi-bin/melcrum/eu_ content.pl?docurl=topic%20km **RSS** http://www.melcrum.com/rss/ feed.xml
8. Montague Institute Review http://www. montague.com/review/review.html **RSS** http://www.montaguelab.com/ digest.xml

Websites

1. CIO KM Research Center http://www. cio.com/research/knowledge/ **RSS** http://www2.cio.com/search/rss/ feed22.xml
2. CPsquare http://www.cpsquare.org/ News/ **RSS** http://www.cpsquare.org/News/ index.rdf
3. Gurteen http://www.gurteen.com/ gurteen/gurteen.nsf/ **RSS** http://www.gurteen.com/gurteen/ gurteen.nsf/id/gurteen-klog.xml
4. ITtoolbox KM Knowledge Base http:// knowledgemanagement.ittoolbox.com/ **Feeds** http://knowledgemanagement. ittoolbox.com/subscriptions/feeds.asp
5. KnowledgeBoard http://www. knowledgeboard.com/index.html **Feeds** http://www.knowledgeboard. com/rss/index.html
6. KNOW Network http://www. knowledgebusiness.com/ **Feeds** http://www.knowledgebusiness. com/knowledgebusiness/Templates/ RssTemplate.aspx

Blogs

1. Patti Anklam – Networks, Complexity, and Relatedness http://www.byeday.net/weblog/ networkblog.html **RSS** http://www.byeday.net/ weblog/rss.xml
2. Tom Baldwin – Knowledgeline http:// kmpipeline.blogspot.com/ **RSS** http://feeds.feedburner.com/ Knowledgeline
3. Steve Barth – Reflexions http:// reflexions.typepad.com/reflexions/ **RSS** http://reflexions.typepad.com/ reflexions/index.rdf
4. Bill Brantley – Eclectic Bill http:// eclecticbill.blogspot.com/

RSS http://feeds.feedburner.com/
blogspot/PUIz

5. Marnix Catteeuw – Knowledge
   Management in Practice http://
   marnixcatteeuw.spaces.live.com/
   RSS http://marnixcatteeuw.spaces.live.
   com/feed.rss

6. Yigal Chamisch – The Knowledge
   Management and Storytelling Blog
   http://yigalc.wordpress.com/
   RSS http://yigalc.wordpress.com/feed

7. Tom Davenport, Larry Prusak and Don
   Cohen (Babson College) – Knowledge
   Work, Management & Productivity
   http://www.babsonknowledge.org/
   RSS http://www.babsonknowledge.org/
   atom.xml

8. Ross Dawson – Trends in the Living
   Networks http://=www.rossdawsonblog.
   com/**RSS** http://www.rossdawsonblog.
   com/index.rdf

9. Keith De La Rue – Tech-know http://
   www.nowwearetalking.com.au/Home/
   PageBlog.aspx?mid=210
   RSS http://www.nowwearetalking.com.
   au/Feeds/nwat_blog_techKnow_rss.xml

10. Steve Denning – The Leader's Guide to
    Storytelling http://stevedenning.typepad.
    com/
    RSS http://stevedenning.typepad.com/
    steve_denning/index.rdf

11. Jon Doctor – KM Now! http://blogs.
    ittoolbox.com/km/now
    RSS http://rss.ittoolbox.com/rss/
    km-now.xml

12. Seth Earley – Not Otherwise Categorized
    http://sethearley.wordpress.com/
    RSS http://sethearley.wordpress.com/feed

13. Lilia Efimova – Mathemagenic http://
    blog.mathemagenic.com/
    RSS http://blog.mathemagenic.com
    /rss.xml

14. Ingo Forstenlechner – ingoblog:
    knowledge management (km) / km

metrics / http://forstenlechner.info/
RSS http://feeds.feedburner.com/
Ingoblawg

15. Stan Garfield – line56.com KM
    Blog http://www.line56.com/blogs/
    contributor_index.asp?ContributorID=1
    RSS http://feeds.feedburner.com/
    Line56comE-businessBlogs

16. Peter-Anthony Glick – Leveraging
    Organizational Knowledge http://
    leveragingknowledge.blogspot.com/
    RSS http://leveragingknowledge.
    blogspot.com/atom.xml

17. Tom Godfrey – Why Knowledge
    Management? http://ykm.typepad.com/
    yerfdogs_knowledge_manage/
    RSS http://ykm.typepad.com/yerfdogs_
    knowledge_manage/index.rdf

18. Denham Grey – Knowledge-at-work
    http://denham.typepad.com/km/
    RSS http://denham.typepad.com/
    km/index.rdf

19. Kelly Ann Green – Crossed Wires http://
    librarygeek.wordpress.com/
    RSS http://librarygeek.wordpress.
    com/feed/

20. John Hagel – Edge Perspectives http://
    www.edgeperspectives.typepad.com/
    RSS http://edgeperspectives.typepad.
    com/edge_perspectives/index.rdf

21. June Holley, Valdis Krebs and Jack
    Ricchiuto — Network Weaving http://
    www.networkweaving.com/blog/
    RSS http://www.networkweaving.com/
    blog/atom.xml

22. Brian Hopkins – Enterprise Knowledge
    Management http://blogs.ittoolbox.
    com/km/hopkins
    RSS http://rss.ittoolbox.com/rss/km-
    hopkins.xml

23. Bruce Hoppe – Connectedness http://
    connectedness.blogspot.com/
    RSS http://connectedness.blogspot.
    com/atom.xml

24. Joitske Hulsebosch – Communities of practice for development http://joitskehulsebosch.blogspot.com/ **RSS** http://feeds.feedburner.com/ CommunitiesOfPracticeForDevelopment

25. Bill Ives – Portals and KM http://billives. typepad.com/portals_and_km/ **RSS** http://billives.typepad.com/portals_ and_km/index.rdf

26. Seth Kahan – collaboratioNation http://collaborationation.typepad.com/ collaborationation/ **RSS** http://collaborationation.typepad. com/collaborationation/index.rdf

27. Dan Kirsch – Dr. Dan's Daily Dose http://blogs.ittoolbox.com/km/dr-dan **RSS** http://rss.ittoolbox.com/rss/ km-dr-dan.xml

28. Nikolay Kryachkov – KnowledgePerson. com http://knowledgeperson. blogspot.com/ **RSS** http://knowledgeperson.blogspot. com/atom.xml

29. Patrick Lambe, Edgar Tan and Paolina Martin – Green Chameleon http:// greenchameleon.com/ **RSS** http://www.greenchameleon.com/ feeds/rss/

30. Jim Lee – APQC's Knowledge Management Blog http://apqckm. blogspot.com/ **RSS** http://apqckm.blogspot.com/ atom.xml

31. John Maloney – Colabria http:// kmblogs.com/public/blog/110296 **RSS** http://kmblogs.com/public/ rss/110296

32. Jim McGee – McGee's Musings http://www.mcgeesmusings. net/index.php **RSS** http://feeds.feedburner.com/ McgeesMusings

33. G. Brett Miller – No Straight Lines http://nsl.gbrettmiller.com/ **RSS** http://feeds.feedburner.com/ GBrettMiller

34. Andrew Mitchell – "What's next?" said the cow http://mitchell.wordpress.com/ **RSS** http://mitchell.wordpress. com/feed

35. Matt Moore – Engineers Without Fears http://engineerswithoutfears. blogspot.com/ **RSS** http://engineerswithoutfears. blogspot.com/atom.xml

36. Luke Naismith – Knowledge Futures http://knowledgefutures. wordpress.com/ **RSS** http://knowledgefutures.wordpress. com/feed/

37. Vijeesh Papulli – Knowledge Management: A Practitioner's View http://kmview.blogspot.com/ **RSS** http://kmview.blogspot.com /atom.xml

38. Dave Pollard – How to Save the World http://blogs.salon.com/0002007/ **RSS** http://blogs.salon.com /0002007/rss.xml

39. Emanuele Quintarelli – InfoSpaces http://www.infospaces.it/wordpress/ RSS http://www.infospaces.it/ wordpress/feed

40. Andrew Rixon, Mark Schenk, and Shawn Callahan – Anecdote http://www. anecdote.com.au/ **RSS** http://feeds.feedburner.com/ Anecdote

41. James Robertson – Column Two http:// www.steptwo.com.au/columntwo/ **RSS** http://www.steptwo.com.au/ columntwo/index.xml

42. Oliver Schwabe – Practitioner Perspectives on Value Networks and Knowledge Innovation http:// oliverschwabe.blogspot.com/ **RSS** http://feeds.feedburner.com/ OliverSchwabe/

43. Euan Semple – The Obvious? http://
theobvious.typepad.com/blog/
RSS http://feeds.feedburner.com/
typepad/CfUv

44. George Siemens – Knowing Knowledge
http://www.knowingknowledge.com/
blog/index.php
RSS http://www.knowingknowledge.
com/atom.xml

45. Dave Snowden – Cognitive Edge http://
www.cognitive-edge.com/
RSS http://www.cognitive-edge.com/
atom.xml

46. Pooja Songar – (Knowledge + Ideas) =
INNOVATION http://poojasongar.com/
blog/
RSS http://poojasongar.com/blog/
?feed=rss2

47. Luis Suarez – E L S U A ~ A KM Blog
http://www.elsua.net/
RSS http://www.elsua.net/feed/

48. Luis Suarez – elsua: The Knowledge
Management Blog http://blogs.
ittoolbox.com/km/elsua/
RSS http://blogs.ittoolbox.com/km/
elsua/index.xml

49. Robert Swanwick – E-Business Blog
http://www.line56.com/articles/story_
index.asp?StoryType=18
RSS http://feeds.feedburner.com/
Line56comE-businessBlogs

50. Dinesh Tantri – Organic KM http://
dineshtantri.blogspot.com/
RSS http://feeds.feedburner.com/
blogspot/organickm

51. Carla Verwijs – Far Wise in
Knowledge Management
http://carlav.blogs.com/km/
RSS http://carlav.blogs.com/km/
index.rdf

52. Jack Vinson – Knowledge Jolt with Jack
http://blog.jackvinson.com/
RSS http://blog.jackvinson.com/
atom.xml

53. Kaye Vivian – Dove Lane
http://dove-lane.com/
RSS http://dove-lane.com/index.php/
?feed=rss2

54. Douglas Weidner – KM Body of
Knowledge http://blogs.ittoolbox.com/
km/bok
RSS http://rss.ittoolbox.com/rss/
km-bok.xml

55. David Weinberger – Joho the Blog
http://www.hyperorg.com/blogger/
index.html
RSS http://www.hyperorg.com/blogger/
index.rdf

56. Nancy White – Full Circle Online
Interaction Blog http://www.fullcirc.com/
weblog/onfacblog.htm
RSS http://www.fullcirc.com/weblog/
feed/atom.xml

57. Terry Yelmene – knowledgeer-at-large
http://www.knowledgeeratlarge.net/
RSS http://www.knowledgeeratlarge.
net/?feed=atom

58. Christian Young – Reflections of
a Knowledge Manager http://
kmreflections.blogspot.com/
RSS http://feeds.feedburner.com/
KMReflections

59. Group Blog – Microsoft Knowledge
Network Team Blog http://blogs.msdn.
com/kn/
RSS http://blogs.msdn.com/kn/atom.xml

60. Group Blog – Talking Knowledge
Management http://talkingkm.
blogspot.com/
RSS http://talkingkm.blogspot.com/
atom.xml

KM conferences
United States

1. Braintrust International KM Summit
http://www.iirusa.com/events/index.
xml?_parent_id=54

2. Delphi Group Information Intelligence Summit http://www.delphigroup.com/events/

3. E-Gov Institute Annual Knowledge Management Conference http://events.fcw.com/

4. APQC Annual Knowledge Management Conference http://www.apqc.org/portal/apqc/ksn/calendar

5. KMWorld and Intranets http://www.kmworld.com/kmw06/

6. ACM Conference on Information and Knowledge Management (CIKM) http://www.cikm.org/

Asia Pacific

1. KM Australia http://www.kmaustralia.com

2. Australia: actKM Conference http://www.actkm.org/conferences.php

3. Malaysia: Knowledge Management International Conference and Exhibition (KMICE) http://kmice.uum.edu.my/

4. Singapore: Information and Knowledge Management Society (iKMS) Conference http://www.ikms.org/

5. Singapore: KM Asia http://www.kmasia.com

6. Korea: World Knowledge Forum http://www.wkforum.org/

7. International Conference on Knowledge Management in Asia Pacific (KMAP) http://www.kmap2006.com/

8. Hong Kong: Asia Pacific Conference on Knowledge Management (APCKM) http://www.hkkms.org/

9. Australian Conference on Knowledge Management and Intelligent Decision Support (ACKMIDS) http://www.infotech.monash.edu.au/research/groups/km/

Europe

1. ECKM: European Conference on Knowledge Management http://www.academic-conferences.org/eckm/eckm-home.htm

2. European Knowledge Management Thought Leaders Forum http://www.kmthoughtleaders.com/

3. International Conference on Knowledge Management (ICKM) http://www.executiveacademy.at/executive-academy-mainsite/seminare?filter=7

4. International Conference on Knowledge Culture and Change in Organizations http://managementconference.com/

5. Knowledge and Content UK (KCUK) http://www.kc-uk.co.uk/

6. Austria: International Conference on Knowledge Management (I-KNOW) http://i-know.know-center.tugraz.at/

7. Austria: Practical Aspects of Knowledge Management (PAKM) http://www.dke.univie.ac.at/pakm2006/

Other

1. International Conference on Intellectual Capital and Knowledge Management (ICICKM) http://www.academic-conferences.org/icickm/icickm-home.htm

2. International Conference on Knowledge Sharing And Collaborative Engineering http://www.iasted.org/conferences/2006/vi/ksce.htm

3. Canada: McMaster World Congress http://worldcongress.mcmaster.ca/

Training

There are many sources of training on KM and related topics. Here are ten sources.

1. Anecdote http://www.anecdote.com.au/courses.php

2. APQC http://www.apqc.org/portal/apqc/site/?path=/services/professionaldevelopment/index.html

3. Ark Group http://www.ark-group.com/home/events/default.asp
4. Delphi Group http://www.delphigroup.com/events/institute/km.htm
5. eKnowledgeCenter KM Professional Development Programme http://www.eknowledgecenter.com/
6. Free KM Training: KM Concepts http://www.km.org/Free_km_eLO/CKMCKEECTC.htm
7. KMCI http://www.kmci.org/
8. KM Institute (International Knowledge Management Institute) http://www.kminstitute.org/index.php
9. KMPro (Knowledge Management Professional Society) http://kmpro.org/static.php?file=training.htm
10. KMWorld Web Events (including KMWorld Web University) http://www.kmworld.com/Webinars/

There are also many local sources of training in languages other than English. For example, in Austria: Knowledge Management Academy KM Master Programme http://www.km-a.net/

In addition, many of the experts listed below offer standard or customised training.

Experts

Here are 52 of the leading KM consultants and authors, in alphabetical order:

1. Verna Allee http://www.vernaallee.com/
2. Debra Amidon http://www.entovation.com/amidon/biographical.htm
3. Patti Anklam http://www.byeday.net/patti.htm
4. Jerry Ash http://www.kwork.org/counsel.html
5. Steve Barth http://reflexions.typepad.com/about.html
6. Nick Bontis http://www.bontis.com/

7. John Seely Brown http://www.johnseelybrown.com/
8. Bob Buckman http://www.gurteen.com/gurteen/gurteen.nsf/id/bob-buckman
9. Shawn Callahan http://www.anecdote.com.au/shawn_callahan.html
10. Chun Wei Choo http://choo.fis.utoronto.ca/
11. Chris Collison http://www.chriscollison.com/
12. Richard Cross http://www.mchglobal.com/about.htm
13. Rob Cross http://www.robcross.org/
14. Tom Davenport http://www.tomdavenport.com/
15. Steve Denning http://www.stevedenning.com/
16. Nancy Dixon http://commonknowledge.org/page.asp?id=29
17. Peter Drucker http://www.peter-drucker.com/
18. Paul Duguid http://ist-socrates.berkeley.edu/~duguid/
19. Seth Earley http://www.earley.com/
20. Leif Edvinsson http://www.gurteen.com/gurteen/gurteen.nsf/id/leif-edvinsson
21. Stan Garfield http://groups.msn.com/KnowledgeManagement
22. Carol Kinsey Goman http://www.ckg.com/
23. Denham Grey http://denham.typepad.com/about.html
24. Kent Greenes http://www.greenesconsulting.com/Kent-Greenes.html
25. David Gurteen http://www.gurteen.com/gurteen/gurteen.nsf/id/about-dg
26. Bruce Hoppe http://connectiveassociates.com/about.html
27. Bill Ives http://billives.typepad.com/about.html
28. Bruce Karney http://km-experts.com/staff.htm
29. Valdis Krebs http://www.orgnet.com/VKbio.html

30. Patrick Lambe http://www.
straitsknowledge.com/about/

31. Martyn Laycock http://www.
managingtransitions.net/profile.htm

32. Dorothy Leonard http://dor.hbs.edu/
fi_redirect.jhtml?facInfo=bio&facEmId=
dleonard&loc=extn

33. Richard McDermott http://www.
mcdermottconsulting.com/about.shtml

34. Fred Nickols http://www.nickols.us/

35. Ikujiro Nonaka http://www.gurteen.com/
gurteen/gurteen.nsf/id/ikujiro-nonaka

36. Carla O'Dell http://www.apqc.org/
portal/apqc/site/?path=/aboutus/
leadership/index.html

37. Geoff Parcell http://www.practicalkm.
com/about_me.htm

38. Dave Pollard http://blogs.salon.
com/0002007/stories/2006/07/05/
aboutTheAuthor.html

39. Larry Prusak
http://www.laurenceprusak.com/

40. Greg Reid http://www.infuture.pro/
about/Introduce/CEO_Profile.html

41. Chris Riemer http://www.
knowledgestreet.com/About_Us/about_
us.html

42. Melissie Rumizen http://www.kwork.org/
Stars/rumizen.html

43. Hubert Saint-Onge http://www.
saintongealliance.com/ourteam.asp

44. Euan Semple http://www.euansemple.
com/

45. David Skyrme http://www.skyrme.com/
dsa/david.htm

46. Dave Snowden http://www.cognitive-
edge.com/whoweare.php

47. Thomas Stewart http://members.aol.
com/thosstew/bio.html

48. Karl-Erik Sveiby http://www.sveiby.com/
KarlErikSveiby/tabid/53/Default.aspx

49. George Von Krogh http://www.
alexandria.unisg.ch/persone/Georg_
Vonkrogh/L-en

50. Jack Vinson http://www.jackvinson.com/
about.html

51. Etienne Wenger
http://www.ewenger.com/

52. Karl Wiig http://www.krii.com/who_we_
are.htm

KM communities

Here are KM communities, discussion lists,
and groups which you can join.

No fees required

■ actKM Discussion List http://actkm.org/
mailman/listinfo/actkm_actkm.org

■ Communities of Practice http://groups.
yahoo.com/group/com-prac/

■ KnowledgeBoard http://www.
knowledgeboard.com/

■ Learning to Fly http://finance.groups.
yahoo.com/group/learning-to-fly/

■ Organizational Network Analysis http://
finance.groups.yahoo.com/group
/ona-prac/

■ Systems Integration KM Leaders
http://tech.groups.yahoo.com/group/
sikmleaders/

■ Taxonomy Community of Practice http://
finance.groups.yahoo.com/group/
TaxoCoP/

■ Value Networks http://groups.google.
com/group/Value-Networks

Fees required for full membership

■ APQC http://www.apqc.org/portal/
apqc/ksn

■ Association of Knowledgework (AOK)
http://finance.groups.yahoo.com/
group/AOK_K-Net/

■ CPsquare http://www.cpsquare.org/

■ Network Roundtable
https://webapp.comm.virginia.edu/
networkroundtable/

- Working Knowledge Research Center at Babson College http://www3.babson.edu/Bee/research/wk/clusters
- Knowledge Management http://www.kmcluster.com/
- Prediction Markets http://www.pmcluster.com/
- Value Networks http://www.vncluster.com/

Local KM communities

- Australia: Brisbane – Queensland Knowledge Management Forum (QKM) http://au.groups.yahoo.com/group/qkm/
- Australia: Canberra – actKM Forum http://www.actkm.com/
- Australia: Melbourne Knowledge Management Leadership Forum (KMLF) http://www.melbournekmlf.org/
- Australia: Sydney – NSW KM Forum http://www.nsw-km-forum.org.au/wiki.pl
- Boston: Boston KM Forum http://www.kmforum.org/
- Chicago: KM Chicago http://finance.groups.yahoo.com/group/kmchicago/
- Hong Kong: Hong Kong KM Society http://www.hkkms.org/
- Japan: KM Society of Japan http://www.kmsj.org/
- Korea: KM Society of Korea http://wcic.kmsk.or.kr/
- London: The London Knowledge Network (LKN) http://www.londonknowledgenetwork.org.uk/
- Michigan: Midwest KM Community http://finance.groups.yahoo.com/group/Midwest_KM_Community/
- Middle East: Arab Knowledge and Management Society (AKMS) http://www.akms.org/
- New Zealand: NZKM – The New Zealand KM Network http://www.nzkm.net/

- North Carolina: KM Network of North Carolina (KMNNC) http://finance.groups.yahoo.com/group/KMNNC/
- Philadelphia: KM Group (KMG) Philadelphia Chapter http://www.kmgphila.org/
- India: KM-Forum http://ncsi.iisc.ernet.in/mailman/listinfo/km-forum
- Malaysia: KMtalk.net http://www.kmtalk.net/index.php
- Singapore: Information and Knowledge Management Society (iKMS) http://www.ikms.org/
- Taiwan: KM Research Center http://www.kmrc.org/
- Toronto: Toronto KM Directors Group http://blogs.salon.com/0002007/categories/businessInnovation/2004/03/18.html
- Various: Gurteen Knowledge Cafés http://www.gurteen.com/gurteen/gurteen.nsf/id/kcafes

KM institute chapters

- Hampton Roads, VA http://www.kminstitute.org/hamptonroadschapter.html
- Kansas City, MO http://www.kminstitute.org/kansascitychapter.html
- Northern New Jersey http://www.kminstitute.org/newjerseychapter.html
- Ottawa, Ontario http://www.kminstitute.org/ottawachapter.html
- Washington, DC http://www.kminstitute.org/washingtondcchapter.html

Index

A